Keeping Sunday
Special

Keeping Sunday Special

The Fight Against The Shops Bill

Dr Michael Schluter
with
David J. Lee

Marshall Pickering

Marshall Morgan and Scott
Marshall Pickering
3 Beggarwood Lane, Basingstoke, Hants RG23 7LP, UK

First published in 1988 by Marshall Morgan and Scott Publications Ltd
Part of the Marshall Pickering Holdings Group
A subsidiary of the Zondervan Corporation

Scripture quotations in this publication are from the Holy Bible, New
International Version. Copyright © 1973, 1978, 1984 International
Bible Society. Published by Hodder and Stoughton.

British Library CIP Data

Schluter, Michael
  Keeping Sunday special.
  1. Great Britain. Retail trades. Opening hours
  I. Title
  381′.1′0941

ISBN: 0 551 01752 X

Text Set in Baskerville by Brian Robinson, Buckingham, England
Printed in Great Britain by Cox and Wyman, Reading

Contents

Acknowledgements

This book has been made possible by the research of David Lee. He drew together the material after interviewing many of the key actors, and carried out the major task of writing up the first draft of the book. He also contributed substantially in analysing the particular congruence of political factors which led to the Government's extraordinary defeat in 1986. I am deeply indebted to him and would like to thank him warmly for his commitment to telling this story.

I would also like to thank the many who gave so freely of their time to discuss their understanding of events and who reviewed parts of the manuscript. So many people played a vital role in the defeat of the Bill that it is impossible to mention all of them by name. There may also be important contributions overlooked simply because they remained out of sight at the time. The campaign was so widespread, and involved so many people, it is hard to assess the various components accurately. To those whose contribution has not been adequately reflected in this book, I ask their indulgence and forgiveness. All errors and omissions remain my responsibility.

The story has not ended. The second act of the drama is about to unfold with the prospect of further legislative initiatives imminent. My hope and prayer is that the ordinary people who rose up to defend one of the oldest institutions in Britain will do so again, and with even greater determination, to counter the threat of new efforts to take away our Sunday.

Michael Schluter
Cambridge
April 1988

This book is dedicated to my wife and children, and to all the many others who sacrificed a small part of their lives in the cause of keeping Sunday special.

Foreword

Dr Michael Schluter is a mighty defender of Sunday as a day of rest, and also as a day for worship by believing Christians. It is above all a family day.

This fascinating story of a small group organising the defeat of the 1987 Shops Bill which sought to make Sunday just like any other day tingles my blood. But this is not the time to sit back and congratulate ourselves that Sunday is safe.

The government are reported to be resolved upon another attempt to change the character of our Sunday. Learning from their past experience they are likely to produce a Bill which gives at least token recognition that Sunday is treasured as a day 'set apart' by the great majority of the British people.

In desperation those who seek to change Sunday legislation pretend that this will be done solely because of the present anomalies in the law. Nothing could be further from the truth. Change is sought not because of anomalies or 'to set people free', but because big profits can be made if Sunday is treated just as a Saturday. Greed is the motive power that inspires the continuous attack on the Christian Sunday.

Michael Schluter has sounded the tocsin for all who cherish Sunday as a very special day. In this book we are warned that the iconoclasts who would turn down every restriction are seeking massive amounts of money from big business to further their propaganda campaign.

All honours to those members of the House of Commons whose rebellion saved the day last time: our task is to be ready to repel the *next* attack which is even now being prepared.

George Tonypandy

Chapter 1

Whose Sunday?

The case was deceptively simple.

The majority of British shoppers, it was claimed, desired the freedom to shop on Sundays. In 1983 the Government had commisioned an Inquiry under the chairmanship of Robin Auld QC to find out if Sunday opening would work. And now, on 20th May 1985 the Home Secretary, Leon Brittan, was standing at the despatch box to recommend that the Report's conclusions be turned into legislation.

'I beg to move', he said, observing the traditional form, 'that this House takes note of the Report of the Committee of Inquiry . . . accepts the case for the removal of legislative limitations on shop hours; and looks forward to the Government bringing forward legislation to remove such limitations.'

It was a sobering prospect. Acceptance of the proposal would authorise the preparation by Government of legislation allowing unprecedented changes not only in retailing but in the whole British way of life. Previous attempts to deregulate Sunday trading had all come in the form of Private Member's Bills, and all had fallen victim to pressure from the lobbies. But Parliamentary analysts agreed that against a Government Bill the lobby was a weapon of straw. The Conservative Government, swept back to power in 1983 with a massive majorioty of 144, hadn't lost a single Bill in six years of office. Even granted the fact that many of their backbenchers strongly resented the use of a three-line whip on what they regarded as a matter of individual conscience, there was no hope of a rebellion drawing enough support for the Auld Committee's recommendations to be rejected.

The deregulation of Sunday trading already looked like a *fait accompli*.

When the Auld Committee presented its Report I knew very little about the deregulation issue.

For seven years I had been working as an economic advisor on agricultural development for the World Bank and the International Food Policy Research Institute. Although I had returned to Britain in 1982 I still spent several months each year on assignments in Africa. Such spare time as I had was taken up with the study of economic issues in Britain, and eventually this led me to set up a small research concern designed to explore the modern application of economic ideas developed in the early Jewish state as outlined in the Old Testament. It was nothing spectacular; I ran it from my office at home in Cambridge, and had two employees – a part-time secretary, and an economics graduate called Chris Townsend whom I'd hired to work on regional policy. Mindful of the Old Testament idea of the fiftieth year, when land was returned to its family owners and slaves were set free, I had named it the Jubilee Centre.

On the strength of my training as an economist I was invited by the Norwich School of Christian Studies in January 1985 to speak about international aid. Although the Christian Lawyers Action Group had asked me before Christmas to write a short paper about the effects of deregulation on family life, I had given little thought to the possible link between deregulation and Old Testament economics, and found myself hard put to respond when after my lecture someone asked me what I thought about Sunday trading.

I replied off the cuff: 'I think it's a more important issue than most of us recognise.'

The questioner then wanted to know if we should be doing something about it.

I hesitated.

'I think we should be praying that God will raise up some person, some institution, to fight the Sunday battle.'

I would have been perfectly content to take my own advice and then, for all intents and purposes, forget about Sunday trading. But the fact was that from the evening I spoke at the Norwich Institute I couldn't get the issue out of my mind; it followed me on the plane to Africa early in February, and dogged me for two whole weeks. By the time I got back I had been forced to admit to myself that I felt called by God to contribute, in some way I did not yet know, to the fight against deregulation. It was no more, or less than that; an obstinate sense of calling.

As soon as I returned to Britain I began to do some research. What I discovered surprised me. Press coverage of the Auld Report – which had in any case been scanty – suggested that Sunday trading was widely supported and that the Government's desire to enshrine the Auld Committee's proposals in legislation was perfectly democratic. But in seeking to remove statutory restrictions on shopping hours, and thus placing the seventh day of the week on a par with the sixth, the Government were not fulfilling an electoral mandate. Nobody had voted them in on the promise to deregulate Sunday trading, for no such commitment had been made. They were in fact using their substantial majority in the Commons to satisfy a demand that had arisen not out of the express wishes of the British people, but from a minority of retail businesses – chiefly in the DIY sector – for whom deregulation was a matter of direct financial gain.

Even granted the power of a right wing ideology, for which market freedom was desirable by definition, the Government's willingness to barter the ancient institution of Sunday for a purpose of so little benefit to the nation as a whole was deeply disturbing. But of course the decision to abolish existing protection against Sunday trading had not been plucked out of the air. The argument had been going on already for many years, just below the horizon of the national media, within the British retail trade. A little further investigation revealed why it had suddenly taken on a wide significance.

Until around 1950 British shoppers were served by a large number of small businesses where, as often as not, the owner himself could be seen behind the counter. A few of these shops had always broken the law on Sunday trading. The infringements were minor, consisting mostly of the sale of a few items not permitted under the Act by shops for which Sunday opening was otherwise quite legal, and abuse did not occur on any noticeable scale until the Retail Revolution of the sixties and seventies placed increasingly large slices of the market into the hands of the multiples.

By the eighties the major multiples were each running hundreds of shops. They had achieved economies of scale sufficient to undercut the prices of most independent retailers with the result that the high streets of Britain's cities and large towns were now dominated by a few famous names. Smaller shops, if they had not been put out of business altogether (and in the grocery trade three-quarters of them had), had either been absorbed by larger rivals, or forced into the suburbs to retain their share of the market. The ownership of retail outlets had fallen into fewer and fewer hands, and in the bid to increase profit margins the atmosphere had grown intensely competitive.

Sunday trading in this situation was not an attractive option for the average shop owner. There were only two ways of expanding your market in retailing; one was to open up some completely new area of demand; the other was to take over a portion of the market that belonged to someone else. Of course – to take a random example – it stood to reason that if one shoe shop opened on a Sunday and all the rest stayed closed, the shop that opened would take some of the trade normally going to other shoe shops from Monday to Saturday. The owner would have pinched a share of somebody else's market. But his advantage would be lost as soon as the other shops opened as well – which they would have to do if they wanted to stay in business – because having an extra day to shop wouldn't necessarily make the customer buy an extra pair of shoes. Six days' trading would just be spread over seven, and everyone would have another day of costs to pay in heat, light and staff wages. This would be especially injurious to the independent shop owner, because for him seven day trading could easily mean seven days standing behind the counter.

In fact Sunday might never have been an issue at all had it not been for the situation of one particular retailing concern – the garden centre. Under the Shops Act 1950 a garden centre that opened on a Sunday could sell little else than cut flowers. The Act thus catered for the immediate needs of visitors to hospitals and graveyards, while prohibiting the sale of merchandise, such as garden forks, hose pipes and trowels, that could reasonably be left until the next day. But there was a problem; because their trade was seasonal, garden centres found it hard to balance the books on the takings of a six day week. Consequently many started to open seven days in spite of the law. That they weren't prosecuted was probably owing to the acceptability of gardening as a Sunday activity, and the untypical nature of the garden centre as a shop. But the apparently permissive attitude of local authorities towards Sunday trading in the gardening business opened up alluring prospects, and gradually garden centres started expanding their stock. In the end it was possible to go to a garden centre on a Sunday afternoon and buy hardware goods, wine and spirits, even carpets.

At this point a twofold reaction started. Some retailers, notably the independent hardware specialists, saw a threat to their markets and looked for the Shops Act to be observed. But others followed suit; DIY merchants, in particular, began to open and so started to cash in on the benefits of Sunday trading. To avoid prosecution, which could as a rule only happen anyway as a result of a specific complaint, the Sunday traders developed some elaborate ruses. One man claimed that wallpaper could be classed as a motor spare if it was used to decorate the inside of a caravan; another sold monstrously expensive carrots with which he gave away free furniture! In any case the fines were so small that many of the larger DIY merchants simply paid up and carried on trading.

Naturally the ripples spread, and it wasn't long before a few of the major multiples were worrying over the threat seven day trading posed to *their* markets. To use an analogy put forward by the John Lewis Partnership, a small number of football supporters had stood up to improve their view of the game, and the rest now had to decide whether to stand up too, or shout until the others sat down. Clearly it wasn't to anyone's advantage to spend the entire match on his feet; but then nobody wanted to lose out by being the only one left sitting down. For retailers operating in a highly competitive climate the choice tended to rest less on principle than on survival. Naturally the out-of-town DIY superstores and multiples with DIY subsidiaries, many of whom were already open on Sundays, came down squarely in favour of changing the law to permit Sunday trading. But even among the retailers who would gain little from being among the first to 'stand up' there was quite often a reluctance to declare their opposition, because if seven day trading became the norm market forces would force them to open whether they liked it or not.

In these circumstances it was hardly surprising that in the debate about implementing the Auld Report Gerald Kaufman described the Retail Consortium, the body representing over ninety percent of British retailers, as sounding a discordant note, rather like the dissonance at the introduction to Mozart's 39th symphony. A few of the businesses within it campaigned actively for deregulation and had formed a pressure group called Open Shop, consisting of W. H. Smith with Do-It-All, Woolworths with B & Q, and three leading groups with furniture interests: Habitat/Mothercare, Harris/Queensway and Asda/MFI. These were opposed by a loose alliance of groups to whom Sunday trading was in some form or another a threat; retailers, many of them representated by the National Chamber of Trade (one of the retail federations in the Consortium); the unions, in particular the Union of Shop, Distributive and Allied Workers (USDAW); and the churches.

So far this second group had been successful in thwarting attempts to liberalise trading hours through Private Members' legislation. Nonetheless there built up over a period of ten years or so – over which some thirteeen of these Bills were brought forward and sunk – an impression of sympathy in the business community to the idea of Sunday trading. This was reinforced in two ways. Firstly through pressure from the consumer organisations, who championed the right of the shopper to shop when he or she wanted to; and secondly, through the inclination of the prevailing political philosophy to give market forces their head. Together all three served to convince the Government that the time had come to step into the fray.

By now everybody was being a little circumspect. Repealing the Shops Act was a major move. Smaller retailers were concerned not to take a position that might offend their customers. Multiples were conscious of the demand of their shareholders for increased turnover and growing profits. And the Government, as governments tend to do, was looking over its shoulder at the electorate. Probably the deregulation of Sunday trading did not have equal appeal to every Minister in the Cabinet; certainly all were aware that turning what was traditionally a matter of conscience into a party political issue by putting it on the Government's legislative agenda was unprecedented and contentious. But with the defeat of the last two Private Members' Bills on Sunday trading – put forward respectively by Baroness Trumpington and Ray Whitney – it seemed the stalemate had to be broken.

So in July 1983 the Home Secretary, Leon Brittan, appointed an Independent Committee of Inquiry under Robin Auld QC to gather evidence from all interested parties and make some recommendation on changes in the law. The Committee had only two other members, Mrs. Liliana Archibald and Miss Frances Cairncross, backed up by six assessors whose job it was to analyse the large quantity of material submitted in due course by, among others, employers, trade unions, churches, consumers and local authorities. Since in the estimate of the Home Secretary none of these groups could produce a comprehensive and impartial review of the economic effects of deregulation, the Auld Committee was assisted in its work by a study specially commissioned from the Institute for Fiscal Studies.

Unfortunately it had long been a truism in Parliamentary circles that the conclusions of a Government Inquiry could be predicted with some accuracy on the basis of the individuals selected to carry it out. Certainly in the case of the Auld Inquiry it was strange, given the generally hostile mood of the Church of England towards Sunday trading, that the assessor chosen to represent the church was clearly in favour of it. But the bias went further than this, for a

19

degreee of momentum for change was even written into the Committee's terms of reference:

> To consider what changes are needed in the Shops Acts, having regard to the interests of the consumers, employers and employees and to the traditional character of Sunday, and to make recommendations as to how these should be achieved.

The real problem, however, did not lie in the membership of the Inquiry, or in its terms of reference, but in the conspicuous gap between the facts it examined and the inferences it drew from them. This was later spelled out unequivocally by one of the Committee's own assessors, Lord Gallacher, who told the Lords that in his view the Committee's findings 'were completely contrary to the evidence they took.' The British Council of Churches said much the same, identifying in a critique of the Committee's work 'a serious conflict between the evidence they present and the conclusion they reach.'

Be that as it may, the Inquiry finished its work, and when the Auld Report arrived on the Home Secretary's desk on 3rd October 1984 its authors had come to a single, flat and unanimous conclusion:

'We are convinced that the removal of restrictions on trading hours offer the best – indeed the only – way forward.'

A few days after my return from a trip to Africa in early February, 1985, I sat down and talked the situation over with my assistant, Chris Townsend.

It was apparent to both of us that the small amount of independent research already done on the Sunday issue was inadequate to challenge the conclusions of the Auld Report. It was too scanty, insufficiently documented. If the Committee's recommendations were to be opposed, therefore, a case would have to be made on the basis of the evidence they themselves had assessed. I asked Chris if he was willing to drop his work on regional policy and take this on as a research project; he agreed. But we both knew research wasn't enough. If the Government committed themselves to act on

20

the recommendations of the Auld Report, as they seemed likely to do when the matter was brought before the Commons in May, we would need not only well-researched arguments but a platform from which to broadcast them. In other words, a campaign.

For me this was *terra incognita*. I knew little about public relations work, and almost nothing about the mysterious business of lobbying MPs. All I had to go on was the vague association – made as I read the Book of Judges on the way back from Africa – of Gideon's 300 men and the 300 or so backbench Conservatives in Parliament: approval of the Auld Report might be a foregone conclusion, but I felt that if we could present just 300 MPs with a persuasive argument against Sunday trading we might influence enough of them to make sure that any legislation brought forward as a result of the Report was not turned into law. Clearly there was more to this than simply writing each MP a polite letter. Something had to be done at local level, something that would prove to an MP not only that there was a case against deregulation, but that the issue mattered to his constituents.

It was probably fortunate at this stage that we had no professional advice; otherwise I would never have begun the arduous task of setting up a constituency network. Cheerfully naive about the scale of the operation I paid a friend, Anne Holmes, to contact church ministers throughout England and Wales, in the hope of discovering enough Christians in each constituency to mount a local campaign. Of course it was a goal hopelessly beyond the reach of one part-time assistant, and that the campaign took off at all was due only to the unexpected appearance of Alasdair Barron.

Alasdair had been working in design and publicity for an agricultural organisation, had been made redundant, and was now pursuing a new job. He called me because a mutual friend knew I had connections in the World Bank. Though I really couldn't think of any openings there I agreed to have lunch with him and talk it over. I was glad I did; I realised as soon as I met him that Alasdair had a gift for organisation; not only that, but he was so determined to stay in employment that he'd agreed, in spite of the low pay, to do an eight week stint developing photographs in Birmingham. I decided to make him an offer; I would employ him on exactly the same terms as the photographic studio if he would come to Cambridge and co-ordinate the campaign. At £2 per hour the rate was hardly generous, but it was all I could afford, and at least it was no less than he'd have got developing prints. If we started to make a little money through the publication of pamphlets there was just the remotest chance of the contract being extended.

Alasdair started work at the Jubilee Centre on 14th April and within three days had instituted an official and minuted staff meeting. Several precedents were set inside the week. The campaign needed a clearly defined goal; to research the issue of Sunday trading and inform the Christian public in such a way that they could make their objections known to their MPs. It needed prayer, both as a feature of its own routine, and as support from the Christian community behind. It also needed to keep Christians informed of developments. Accordingly, the decision was taken to draft, along with some leaflets on deregulation, a prayer letter for the constituency co-ordinators.

We debated long and hard over possible names for the campaign, but didn't select one until the decision was forced on us by the need to identify ourselves on our publications. With a 5pm deadline to meet, and still unable to make up my mind, I received a visit from a friend called Dave Reynolds who had worked in media and PR, and as a result of an hour's discussion there emerged the title 'Keep Sunday Special'. It stuck, and took its familiar form in the logo not long afterwards as a result of our consultation with a small Christian graphics firm, Apple Art.

The time I took Alasdair on was the time when the Jubilee Centre ceased to be a personal hobby and turned into a major exercise in faith. From then on meetings were held regularly every Thursday morning at 9.30. Alasdair quickly made himself indispensible and though we now teetered on the edge of insolvency it was his management that enabled us, by the time the Auld Report was debated in Parliament, to make a reasonable start in the fight to preserve statutory protection for Britain's Sunday. By 20th May when the debate to accept the Report in principle took place, we had sent briefing packs to thirteen MPs, mailed 250 constituencies, recruited twenty co-ordinators, and printed 10,000 campaign cards.

Leon Brittan began his defence of the Auld Report on a point that, fundamentally, no one questioned.

'Shop opening hours were last considered in depth by this House during the debate on the Bill introduced in 1983 by my Honourable Friend the Member for Wycombe. By then it was clear that there was hardly anyone who considered the present state of the law satisfactory. In the first place, it was universally felt that the present distinctions between what could be sold on Sunday and what could not be sold were so arbitrary and outdated as to be indefensible . . .'

This was true. Most people who had looked into the question did not consider the existing legal distinctions to be either sensible or constructive. By law you could buy fish and chips on a Sunday only if you didn't buy them from a fish and chip shop; you could buy oysters only if it was before 10am and you were in 'a state of emergency'. Most notoriously – because it had been drawn attention to *ad nauseum* in the media – you could buy pornographic magazines, but not a Bible.

But the Home Secretary's next statement was not quite fair.

'It was not just a question,' he said, 'of a few items that were on the wrong side of the dividing line. There no longer appeared to be a rational dividing line at all.'

In fact the Shops Act 1950 (which together with one or two minor acts and subsequent case law governed trading hours in England and Wales) had at least two 'rational dividing lines': need and perishability. The first catered for the consumer by recognising a category of essential goods. The second catered for the supplier by allowing to be sold on Sunday such items as would suffer through being left on the shelf until Monday – hence newspapers, and by extension all kinds of magazines from the *Beano* to *Playboy*, were exempted from the Act's general prohibition because, like fruit, they were only saleable for a limited period.

What undermined the law was not the lack of a rational basis for distinction, but the inability of the distinctions themselves to keep abreast of the times. In the early twentieth century, for instance, when much of the detail preserved in the 1950 Act was first drawn up, the provision for a traveller to buy hay for his horse was only practical – no Edwardian would carry a bale of hay around with him, any more than a modern motorist carried a complete set of spares. Subsequent Acts had made adjustments to accommodate the needs of the motorist, but many of the ancient and now baffling provisions remained.

It was these, rather than any inherent weakness in the structure of the 1950 Act, which had earned it the popular reputation in the press of being, in the words of Peter Wilsher (writing later in the *Sunday Times*, 23rd February 1986):'nonsensical, contradictory and almost unenforceable'. Significantly, Leon Brittan did not base his objections to it on any inconvenience anomalies might cause to the public. There was no clamour for change, after all, from worshippers outraged that they could not purchase a Bible on the way to church, or from motorists who found it offensive to fill their cars at a petrol station frequented by the local riding club. His point was rather that an irrelevant law was apt to be disregarded; '. . . the law is being regularly, flagrantly and publicly flouted up and down the country', and,' . .As a minister whose primary responsibility is for law and order, I could not advise the House to let the present position remain unaltered'.

How regular and flagrant the flouting really was deserved some thought. At any rate, Gerald Kaufman, the shadow Home Secretary, wasn't impressed by the argument that unpopular laws should be done away with.

'Does that mean that, as we now have the greatest outbreak of robbery known in the history of our country, the Government will remove the laws against Robbery? . . . Does it mean that where the law is sufficiently broken, the Home Secretary will not seek to uphold it but will change it to suit those who broke the law?'

Leon Brittan replied drily, 'As the right honourable Gentleman has put his remarks in the form of questions, I shall answer them. He knows perfectly well the difference between a law that is broken and a law that is unacceptable because it is no longer one that the majority of people want.'

This was a slightly different point, and it raised two

important questions. First, if abolition of the Shops Act was indeed what the 'majority of people' wanted, did that put Parliament under moral obligation to abolish it? What about the laws governing the speed limit? If every driver in the country wanted to raise the speed limit to 100 mph that alone would not be sufficient to cause to change the law. It would also need to be demonstrated that a higher speed limit did not, for instance, prejudice the safety of drivers or pedestrians – a matter distinct from that of the public will. The worthiness of a law, and its popularity, were two different things.

The second question concerned the inherent truth of the assertion. It was quite certain that the 'majority of people' had not spontaneously lobbied their MPs to demand seven day trading. Insofar as their opinion had been consulted at all it was on the basis of polls and surveys commissioned by other groups that had, in many cases, independent reasons for wanting to show that public opinion was behind them. This annexing of the supposed popular will to the Government's cause had become a familiar feature of the dispute over Sunday trading, and the Home Secretary would not hear it denied before the crucial vote on the Auld Report.

The debate went on for several hours. We had known all along there was no possibility of the Government being defeated, and were more interested in discovering signs of a Conservative backbench rebellion which might be built on between the Auld debate and the time when deregulation came back to the Commons in the form of a Government Bill. Chris had predicted that perhaps thirty Conservative backbenchers would defy the Whips and vote against the motion, with another thirty abstaining. As things turned out this was optimistic. I was away in Africa with the World Bank on the day of the debate, and had to phone Alasdair from Nairobi early Tuesday morning to hear the result.

The Government had won by 120 votes.

Chapter 2

The Churches Militant

The need for grassroots support/The Pro Sunday Coalition/Your Sunday is about to be Hijacked/Sabbatarians and Sabbatarianism/The Sabbath and Sunday/Is Sunday worth saving?

Not surprisingly, Leon Brittan considered the result 'Clear cut, and very gratifying.' The Home Office would now draft a Bill. If everything went according to plan the deregulation of Sunday trading would presumably be mentioned in the Queen's speech in November and the Bill presented to Parliament before Christmas. That meant it would be on the Statute Books not later than the middle of 1986.

Stopping it was, on any reckoning, virtually impossible. The Government had an overall majority in the Commons of 140, and if the debate on the Auld Report was anything to go by they wouldn't be afraid to impose the threeline whip a second time. So even assuming that the other parties turned out in force to vote against the Bill, which was by no means certain, we were left with the daunting task of persuading almost fifty more Conservative MPs than had rebelled the last time to vote against their own leadership.

We knew right from the start that no amount of research by the Jubilee Centre would achieve that. Producing arguments against Sunday trading was essential, but arguments alone would not be sufficient to make the average Member of Parliament change his mind. Voting against the party leadership was not the best way to recommend yourself for high office, so no sensible MP was going to do it without a good reason. And it seemed that good reasons in politics often had less to do with the merits of a particular case than the effect it was having in the constituencies. We had to

26

show beyond reasonable doubt that Sunday trading was not only bad policy, but unpopular policy. Which meant, in effect, that the success of the campaign hardly depended on us at all; we could shout and bawl as much as we liked about the mischiefs of deregulation – it would make no difference whatever unless a substantial portion of the general public took the trouble to say they agreed with us. If the battle was going to be won, it had to be won by ordinary people. There was no other way.

Several denominations were already making statements to indicate a groundswell of opinion in the Christian church against Sunday trading. A resolution had been passed by the Free Church Federal Council and the British Council of Churches saying that Sunday should be a day for families to be together. Sunday trading was on the agenda for the Church of England General Synod, and in fact on 10th July Synod members approved by an incredible 367-1 a motion 'strongly deprecating' the Government's moves to deregulate Sunday trading and calling on all Christians to resist them. (It might have been 367-2, but John Gummer, the Conservative Party chairman and Synod member for St Edmundsbury and Ipswich, was not present at the debate. The identity of the one dissenter was a matter for speculation.) The Auld Report had not passed unnoticed by the Roman Catholic Church, either; later in the year the Bishops' Conference of England and Wales issued a press release calling for a free vote in the next Parliamentary debate, warning that 'The character of Sunday is threatened by the Government proposals to remove all restrictions on Sunday trading.'

But official church statements were one thing; grassroots response was another. Accordingly at the end of May I contacted a number of Christian organisations with a view to co-ordinating prayer and action at the congregational level. There was a ready response, and Charlie Colchester of CARE – which had already developed a strong interest in the issue – offered to serve as chairman for what soon became Pro Sunday Coalition. Although its committee represented a wide range of Christian opinion the resulting tension was constructive. The common ground of objection to the commercialisation of Sunday soon issued in an invitation to publicity consultant Peter Meadows to assist in the production of a leaflet based on research Chris Townsend at the Jubilee Centre was now completing on the Auld Report. We discussed at some length Peter's idea that we put on the front of the leaflet – *Your Sunday is About To Be Hijacked* – a cartoon of Margaret Thatcher brandishing a machine gun and back up its release by asking an impressionist to do a real-life demonstration. It was dropped for two reasons; one, it would probably detract from the arguments the leaflet was intended to put across, and two, if we were going to win the battle over Sunday trading, we felt we should win it without attacking personalities – a decision that in fact governed all future publicity. We settled in the end for a cover sprayed with bullet holes; a rather limp compromise, as it turned out, because more than one recipient of the leaflet thought they were aspirins!

Notwithstanding, no less than a million copies of *Your Sunday is About To Be Hijacked* were distributed over the summer of 1985. Its phenomenal success was probably owing to its simplicity; the leaflet explained clearly and briefly the principal arguments against deregulation, and asked the reader to do one thing: write to his or her MP. What it managed to do was mobilise the Evangelical wing of the church, in all the denominations. That would not have been possible ten years earlier; the fact that it was possible in 1985 is largely thanks to the influence of writers like John Stott, who had encouraged active Christian political lobbying in the release of the Siberian Seven. At any rate the idea of a campaign began to take root in numerous congregations, and informed letters started arriving in quantity at MPs offices in Westminster.

But by the autumn this had led to an unforseen problem. A Mac cartoon, published in the *Daily Mail* a little later in the year (4th November 1985) illustrated the point perfectly.

The picture showed an Anglican bishop in full regalia leaning casually against the counter of a greengrocer's shop. His two henchmen, wearing stoles and dark glasses and smoking cigarettes, loitered silently at the door as the Bishop extended his crook and yanked the proprietor's head close to his own. 'Nice place you've got here, squire' he remarked. 'We'd hate to see a tempest, pestilence or a plague of locusts come in if the doors were open on a Sunday. . .'

Mac portrayed what was becoming the popular conception of the anti-Sunday-trading lobby: if not exactly an ecclesiastical mafia, then certainly a collection of spoilsports out to wreck the freedom and leisure of the British public. Opposing deregulation made you an anachronism; opposing deregulation and also going to church made you a *Sabbatarian*.

The assumption behind the Sabbatarian label – an assumption evidently swallowed with glib naivity by most of the media – was that all Christian objections to Sunday trading boiled down to religious prejudice. Never mind the smokescreen of concern for the exploited shop assistants; all the Sabbatarian was really out to do was make Sunday as miserable for everyone else as it was for him. Such was the most extreme secular interpretation of Sabbatarianism, and stated in those terms, of course, it was little more than a caricature. Still, it was important to get across that only a small minority of the church in Britain was Sabbatarian (in the true sense of regarding Sunday as equivalent to the Jewish Sabbath) and that even this real Sabbatarianism was not part of the official philosophy of the campaign. The Christian's objections to Sunday trading were for the most part built on a completely different foundation.

By saying that God rested on the seventh day of creation, and blessed the seventh day and made it holy, the Bible did not imply a command to observe the Sabbath any more than it commanded marriage through the story of Adam and Eve. Both were ordinances of creation, institutions for the welfare and good of man which God had built into the universe. In fact the seven day rhythm of work and rest was so satisfactory that attempts to improve on it, made after both the French and Russian revolutions, failed dismally. But from the point of view of the creation narrative they failed only in practical terms; to find any notion of Sabbath-breaking as disobedience to God it was necessary to look further then Genesis.

Observance of the Sabbath day became a legal requirement at the giving of the Ten Commandments: 'Remember the Sabbath day by keeping it holy . . .' Two points had to be noted here. Firstly, unlike the creation ordinances, the Commandments were addressed specifically to Israel. In fact

29

the Sabbath itself was a sign of God's covenant with the nation, and as such it took on a role far beyond its function as a day of rest; its importance paralleled that of a wedding ring, and just as no husband of wife caring about the marriage relationship would throw away the ring, so no conscientious Jew would fail to observe the Sabbath (see Exod. 31:12-18; Ezek. 20:11-12). Secondly, the command to observe the Sabbath expressed God's will for the social order. The account in Deuteronomy, for instance, reminded the Israelites that the Sabbath was binding also for the servants.

> Observe the Sabbath day by keeping it holy, as the Lord your God has commanded you. Six days you shall labour and do all your work, but the seventh day is a Sabbath to the Lord your God. On it you shall not do any work, neither you, nor your son or daughter, nor your manservant or maidservant, nor your ox, your donkey, or any of your animals, nor the alien within your gates, so that your manservant and maidservant may rest, as you do. Remember that you were slaves in Egypt and that the Lord our God brought you out of there with an almighty hand and an outstretched arm, therefore, the Lord your God had commanded you to observe the Sabbath day.
>
> Deut. 5:12-15

The footnote referring to Israel's own former state of slavery was a terse reminder that privilege was not to be taken for granted, and that people in a state of economic dependency were to be treated with respect. In this sense the Sabbath worked as a kind of 'Employee Protection Act' – a principle worth remembering in view of the Auld Committee's remark that 'a statutory provision specifically protecting shopworkers from being required to work against their will on Sundays and late at night would be impracticable. . .' Economic efficiency left to its own devices would always demand that employees work when and as they were needed, and in the long run this could not help but run foul of another important priority for public policy – safeguarding families from undue economic pressure.

Of course the Sabbath of the Old Testament could not be

tansplanted directly into the New. But that did not make it irrelevant; and the commentators who blithely insisted that 'the Sabbath was made for man, not man for the Sabbath', as though this were a *carte blanche* to dispense with the day of rest, underestimated the strength of the Sabbath tradition in Christian faith and practice. Jesus himself – the 'Lord of the Sabbath' – certainly observed it insofar as he gave priority to acts of worship (see Luke 4:16) and acts of mercy (see Mark 3:16). And his re-ordering of man and Sabbath was to be understood not in the context of the liberal attitudes of modern Britain, but against the extremism of the Pharisees – in comparison to whom, even the caricature of today's Sabbatarian grew distinctly pale. In effect Jesus was placing God's laws in a hierarchy; he never sought to abolish or degrade the Sabbath, only to show that when the command to rest came into conflict with the command to love, the latter should take precedence; 'I desire mercy, and not sacrifice' – a caveat which surely applied to the modern observance of Sunday.

Naturally, it could be argued that Jesus, as a Jew, was going to take a more sympathetic view of the Sabbath than could be expected of today's gentile church. A Christian would not regard the Sabbath as a sign of the covenant; the early church quickly abandoned the Jewish Sabbath in favour of the 'first day of the week', a day on which to celebrate their deliverance, by Christ's resurrection, from the slavery of sin and death, as the Jewish Sabbath celebrated Israel's deliverance in Egypt. Nor did any passage in the Epistles, or even in the Gospels, treat the observance of a Sabbath or special day as mandatory. For Paul, the matter was placed firmly in the realm of individual conscience:

One man considers one day more sacred than another; another man considers every day alike. Each one should be fully convinced in his own mind. He who regards one day as special, does so to the Lord. He who eats meat, eats to the Lord, for he gives thanks to God; and he who abstains, does so to the Lord and gives thanks to God.
Romans 14:5-6

31

The situation confronting Christians in Rome, however, differed in one crucial respect from the situation in modern Britain. Christians then were a minority in an essentially pagan culture. Presumably many of them would not have had the freedom to observe the Sabbath even if they had wanted to, and perhaps Paul's advice reflects that constraint.

We were more fortunate. We lived in a country with a Judao-Christian heritage, and consequently the question for us was not whether we should keep Sunday special as a matter of individual conscience, but whether it was important for Britain *as a society* to maintain Sunday as a social institution. British Christians were able to observe Sunday by a happy coincidence of conscience and national tradition; but since Christians were in the minority even in Britain, the rest of the population would have every right to complain if we tried to foist Sunday on them just because it was important to us. Sunday had to be proven a good and useful institution for society at large – a case for which there was fortunately no lack of supporting evidence.

So although the Christian support of Sunday as a special day had to take account of the opportunity it gave believers to do what had always been the purpose of the Jewish Sabbath – namely, to love the Lord our God with all our heart, all our mind, all our soul, and all our strength – so far as the campaign was concerned, the Sabbath tradition furnished at least three other reasons to fight against the deregulation of Sunday trading:

One, following the principle of the Sabbath as a creation ordinance, Sunday provided a welcome rhythm to British life – after all, most people looked forward to their weekends.

Two, following the principle behind the Sabbath law as stated in Exodus, Sunday helped to preserve family and community life by ensuring that members were given the chance to be off work and together at the same time.

Three, following the principle behind the Sabbath law as stated in Deuteronomy, Sunday afforded some protection to lower paid employees against the pressure to work seven days a week.

For the Auld Report, of course, the moral benefits of Sunday were only factors to be weighed in the balance against the economic advantages of deregulation; and ultimately they were found wanting. It was argued firstly that the day of rest had less relevance in 1985 than it had in ancient Israel, and secondly that changing social and economic circumstances carried with them an obligation to adjust blindly the pattern of national life. Personally I doubted the first contention and distrusted the second. But the Auld Committee had made a case for deregulation, and the survival of Sunday in Britain now depended in great measure on how fast and effectively we could attack the Auld Committee's recommendations.

Chapter 3

Why Auld was Wrong

Why Keep Sunday Special?/The law on Sunday trading: anomalous, complicated, disregarded?/Economic effects of deregulation/The theory of freedom/Sunday trading and the family, the shopworker, the disadvantaged, the feel of the day, the churchgoer.

During the summer of 1985 we took on a number of students to help with the mailing and phoning. The demand for information was growing rapidly, and as we were forced to process and send out more and more material, so the operation had to spill out of my office and into the garage. One of the students, Tim Law, took over the co-ordination of the constituency network, which freed Alasdair to concentrate on the publication of the Jubilee Centre's original research. His simultaneous planning of a number of publications had the curious result that when Chris Townsend's research on the Auld Report became the first piece of work to be put into print (as *Why Keep Sunday Special*) it bore the superscription *Jubilee Centre Paper No. 5*.

In fact the implications of Chris' study had been clear at an early stage. When Leon Brittan recommended the Auld Report in the Commons, his first point was that the Shops Act 1950 was riddled with anomalies, and was therefore a bad law. To an extent that was true; it was clearly an anomaly, for instance, for the sale of gin to be legal when the sale of dried milk was not. But the cry for the anomalous law to be done away with needed to be put in context. To give one example: the fact that takeaway coffee sold hot was subject to VAT while the same cup of coffee, cold, was exempt, had never been put forward as a reason for abolishing VAT. Similarly, the Auld Report's judgement of the Shops Act as

34

'not easy for a lawyer to understand . . . let alone the average shopkeeper' was nonsense; the problem lay not in interpreting the list, but in keeping it up to date. 'Anomalous' and 'complicated' were thus relative terms. But even if the Shops Act was more anomalous and complicated than most other laws, that in itself did not prove the case for abolition. Which was why the Home Secretary followed up the point by stressing that the present shopping hours legislation was not only bad law, but that law openly flouted by retailers.

He took this cue directly from the Auld Report, which asserted that the law 'is widely disregarded by shopkeepers all over the country'. The Auld Report, however, presented no evidence in support of this claim; there was in fact no evidence available either to support or refute it. True enough, the National Consumer Council had made much of the claim that, in an analysis of local press advertising carried out by a press cutting agency for one month in 1983, there were no less than 1,694 advertisements for shops which opened illegally. But placed in the context of the total number of local papers in Britain (estimated at 2,095) this actually worked out at less than one advertisement per month per newspaper. Another smallscale study conducted in Cardiff, which monitored food and grocery purchases, yielded the rather more impressive statistic that 42.1 percent of Sunday purchases were of illegal products. Yet this too has to be set in context, and that researchers admitted that for Sundays 'average expenditure across the twenty-four weeks accounted for less than one percent of total weekly expenditure . . .'

Neither result proved much about the general pattern of Sunday opening. After talking this over, Chris and I decided it would be in the interests of our case for the Jubilee Centre to carry out a survey aimed at discovering the extent of illegal Sunday trading. We did this over a four month period between 10am and 1pm on Sunday mornings, selecting forty-four locations (eleven in London, the rest as far apart as Newcastle and Plymouth) to represent a diversity of settlement types. Although we deliberately restricted our sample to the retailing centres, and so excluded the out-of-town DIY stores, the results were revealing; of more than 12,000 shops surveyed only eight percent were open, and of these three-quarters were complying almost entirely with the law.

This added weight to the view that far from being 'regularly, publicly and flagrantly flouted' the law was held in respect by the vast majority of British shopkeepers. Fewer than one in fifty came anywhere near disregarding the regulations on the scale suggested by Leon Brittan. There was certainly nothing to substantiate the view that opposing deregulation was a feeble attempt to close the stable door after the horse had bolted. On what basis, then, could deregulation be justified?

Apparently not on the basis of its economic effects. The Auld Report conceded that if retail turnover was going to rise, then either people would have to increase their overall spending or they would have to direct a greater proportion to the retail sector of what they spent already. Seven day trading seemed unlikely to have either effect. The freedom to shop in the evenings and on Sunday might siphon a small amount of spending away from things like package holidays and into the purchase of consumer items; and there might be a slight increase in the amount of money spent by foreign tourists. But even the Auld Report admitted that this would add at most only one or two percent to present turnover – and this had to be balanced against the prediction of the Institute of Fiscal Studies (IFS) that a retailer opening for eight hours on Sunday would, under present conditions, add nearly twenty-two percent to his total labour costs. In other words, the short term benefits of deregulation for most retailers would be heavily outweighed by the costs. The result reduced profit margins and, ultimately, increased prices.

In the view of the IFS, the long term prospects from Sunday trading were a little brighter. Over ten years or more, they suggested, costs in the retail trade could be two percent lower with Sunday trading than without; and if this were fully passed on in price reductions to the consumer, the Retail Prices Index would be lowered by 0.4 percent. It was a big 'if'. Also, for the retail sector such benefits as might accrue from deregulation would be unequally distributed. Many DIY stores were already pulling in a quarter of their weekly income on a Sunday; so a company like B&Q, with annual profits of around £30 million, could expect to benefit from deregulation to the tune of five or ten million pounds per annum. For the rest the result of Sunday opening would be a tougher competitive environment in which the weakest – the small, independent traders – would be the first to go to the wall.

The only economic effect the Auld Committee had backed with any conviction was that on employment. The IFS model had predicted that Sunday opening would generate a demand for labour on Sunday 'equivalent' to 73,000 full-time jobs – offset in the short run by losses in weekday jobs. Unfortunately, however, the IFS were at pains to point out that the 'estimation of likely employment effects is extremely problematic, so that precise estimates are impossible to obtain'. This was because changes in employment in the retail sector ultimately depended on the impact of Sunday trading on sales. Significantly, in their original report the IFS had assumed no increase in sales, which in the long run produced a job loss of 20,000. It was only in a second report, carried out under a grant from the Federation of Multiple Hardware DIY Retailers – who were lobbying hard for unrestricted Sunday trading – that they considered the effect of a two percent sale *increase*, and predicted a long term gain of 9,000 jobs. The detriment that increased spending in the retail sector might cause to employment levels in other areas of the economy was not explored.

The most striking conclusion of Chris' analysis of the Auld Report was that the case for deregulation did not rest primarily on legal or economic considerations but on the notion of 'freedom'.

This could be broken down into two propositions. The first, expressing the prevailing political philosophy, was that the interests of society are best served by a general submission to market forces. Clearly the existing Shops Act stood in the way of this. As Leon Brittan said at the end of his speech on 20th May: 'restrictions on the freedom of traders to trade and customers to buy what they want, when they want, are inconsistent with the development of a free economy'. Economic freedom, then, the freedom to buy and sell, was necessary to the efficient working of the market. But this went hand in hand with a second proposition; that freedom was inherently a good thing. The two were linked neatly some time later by Lord Harris of High Cross in *The House Magazine* (7th February 1986): 'For my money, the overwhelming case for the Bill is based on a philosophic preference for freedom of choice and the economic imperative of flexibility and adaptation to social change.'

Both ideas, of course, were theoretical and open to criticism. Certainly the independent retailers were distinctly nervous at the prospect of the market's guiding hand putting them in direct seven day competition with the multiples. For countless small owner/proprietors the cost in social as well as financial terms would be devastating – such people often worked on Sunday already, to catch up on accounts and VAT, and many of them had said openly that they would go into liquidation rather than take on a seven day working week. Consequently, however benign the influence of the free market on society as a whole, no one could pretend that it automatically worked to the advantage of each individual member. In pure form, the free market had no built-in mechanism for ensuring a just distribution of the output it generated. Quite apart from the vagaries of chance, differences in natural ability and resources would inevitably polarise the rich and the poor, from which point onwards the free market tended to favour the rich. Naturally it could be argued that there were trickledown effects, where the wealth of one individual generated work for another, and that British society anyway possessed a number of checks and balances to prevent unlimited wealth and grinding poverty. But the IFS had shown that Sunday trading would have a neglible effect on employment. So why do away with one of the safeguards?

Because people should have freedom of choice. This was the classic philosophy of liberalism; the aim of extending personal freedom – freedom from coercion by others – to the maximum possible degree. The problem with it was that freedom could be expressed in a number of different spheres – moral, economic, intellectual, social, political – and that these were roped together in such a way that greater freedom in one sphere could make it easier or harder to achieve freedom in another. For example, David Tench, Legal

Officer for the Consumer's Association, wrote in *The House Magazine* (7th February 1986): 'The consumer position is clear. Shops ought to be able to open when consumers want to shop'. He was demanding the economic freedom for shoppers to shop when they like – a position also taken (for different reasons) by the Open Shop Group. A statutory gain in freedom for the consumer would not be one for the shopworker, for Sunday trading would without doubt be a great inconvenience to shopworkers who wished to put their faith and family first.

All this raised a profound question about the function of law. The Auld Committee had started from the premise that 'the law should not interfere in the conduct of human affairs unless it serves a justifiable purpose . . . in doing so'. It wasn't hard to see why this idea, yoked with a deep respect for the ideology of the free market, led them to conclude that deregulation was the only way forward. Compared with the soaring ideal of 'freedom' any reasons the evidence suggested for interference by the law looked paltry and mean. But this was a narrow view of the law; as soon as you regarded it as the law's function to promote good for society and restrain harm, the unleashing of the 'freedom' of deregulation in the market place began to look irresponsible if not downright callous.

Chris had isolated three main areas of damage that would be caused by unrestricted Sunday trading.

The first was the family. It was simply a fact that the family – not the state, the courts, the company or the school – occupied pride of place as Britain's central social institution. There was also an undeniable link between family and social breakdown. As early as 1965 an established body of evidence existed to show that parental deprivation was associated with problems in children's emotional development and long term mental health; and this was worrying in view of the fact that the rising divorce rate (it went up by a factor of five in the sixties and seventies) had by 1980 contributed heavily to produce an estimated 890,000 one parent families. Evidently the pressures on family life in Britain were greater than they had ever been before.

To assist analysis of the social consequences of Sunday trading the IFS had predicted that on any one Sunday 350,000 shopworkers would be needed. They reached the figure by taking the average number of shopworkers at work on a weekday, about half the total 2.2 million; this number was halved to reflect their assumption that on a Sunday enough shops would be open to account for just under fifty percent of total retailing capacity, and reduced further on a second assumption that the shops most likely to open would be the least labour intensive. Even on this reasoning 350,000 was almost certain to be an underestimate. If you assumed a rather larger proportion of shops opening after a few years, and then took into account the likelihood that Sunday work would be operated on a rota system, the number of families affected in one way or another quickly topped a million. And that wasn't including the extra labour demanded in ancillary services, such as public transport, waste disposal, policing, traffic supervision, shop inspection, wholesale distribution and so on.

The unavoidable conclusion was that a very large number of families would have their Sunday disrupted by the employment of one or more members of the household. In many cases it would be the wife (since nearly half of the total retailing labour force was made up of married women) and very often a teenage son or daughter. It had been argued in some quarters that this would make little difference to family stability. Frankly, that was hard to believe. Other work patterns that reduced interaction within families had already been proved detrimental. In Young and Wilmot's study of Greater London (*The Symmetrical Family*, 1973) fifty-two percent of shift workers and thirty-four percent of weekend workers had said their work interfered with home and family (the corresponding figure for other workers was twenty-seven percent); and in a study by Elliot on the effects of workload on the family life of junior doctors, seventy-one percent of the wives interviewed reported suffering loneliness as a result of 'limitations on husband-wife interaction'.

The Auld Report nonetheless bravely maintained that the overall effect of Sunday trading on family life would be advantageous. 'Some wives and mothers', they claimed, 'who are tied to the house with children all week may find relief in escaping to a different environment on a Sunday . . .' In fact, 'Sunday shopping has much to offer the family . . . many find that Saturday is not a good day for the kind of shopping that involves the whole family, for household goods, things for the garden, presents and clothes. It is often only on Sundays that they can all get together to make shopping outings of that sort. It must be good for them to be able to spend time together in a leisurely and relaxed way, discussing projects and purchases of interest to them all.'

The wistfully romantic atmosphere evoked in this final sentence was oddly reminiscent of a TV commercial. It certainly bore little resemblance to real life. For a start, how many purchases really involved 'the whole family'? Children weren't known for their interest in purchasing 'household goods' and 'things for the garden'; in the vast majority of these cases they came shopping only because they couldn't be left at home. And as for the 'leisurely and relaxed' style in which these Sunday shoppers were supposed to go about their business, that was dependent on there being few enough shops open (and few enough people in them) for movement to be easy and non-stressful – a condition that would change rapidly as Sunday trading increased. A survey carried out by the Jubilee Centre had already shown a marked increase in shop opening on Good Friday; of shops that had been trading for over ten years the proportion open on Good Friday had risen between 1975 and 1985 from 23 percent to 42.2 percent. Since Good Friday opening was legal, it made a good test case for what might happen to Sunday in the wake of deregulation. Would a Sunday shopping trip with almost half the stores trading really be 'leisurely and relaxed'? It seemed unlikely.

There was an irony in the Auld Committee's final appeal to the social benefits of Sunday trading. They rightly drew attention to the growing number of people living alone, without or far away from families. For them, and for families too sometimes, 'the traditional Sunday' can be a boring, lonely day. The opportunity to shop or work in a shop, or simply to see some life in the shopping high street, may offer a real improvement to the day.' Of course there was some truth in this. But while Sunday trading would certainly act as a palliative for some lonely people, it would increase the loneliness of others – particularly the single elderly – by occupying those who might otherwise have visited them. More important, it would actually exacerbate the social trends that were pressurising family cohesion and making loneliness a problem in the first place.

Of course the effect of Sunday trading on the family would be indirect. But others would suffer the consequence of deregulation first-hand, and none more so than the shopworkers.

It wasn't surprising that the plight of the shopworkers had occupied almost the whole of Gerald Kaufman's speech against the Auld Report. There was a real danger that if the Shops Act were repealed Sunday work would, to all intents and purposes, become compulsory. The majority of submissions to the Committee which addressed the subject had urged that some ruling be made to prevent this, and the National Consumer Council, who were strongly in favour of deregulation, nonetheless confirmed this to be reflective of public opinion as gauged by their surveys; 'Respondents felt very strongly that staff should not be forced to work on Sunday. . .'

Although the Auld Report indicated mixed feelings on the issue among shop staff, Leon Brittan gave no guarantees. In his speech he had merely undertaken to 'look sympathetically at the best way of ensuring that established shopworkers cannot be compelled to work on Sundays' – a thinly veiled warning that even if he did come up with suitable legislation, future generations of shopworkers would not stand to gain from it. In fact there was a real dilemma here. The Auld Committee had hit the mark when they pointed out that statutory protection of this sort would be 'impracticable'; it would be hard to prove, for instance, that a job candidate had been turned down, or that an existing shopworker was denied promotion, purely on account of his or her refusal to work on a Sunday. Possibly such cases would not arise if there were an ample supply of volunteers. But that did not seem likely, for two reasons.

Firstly, the fact that there were volunteers now for work on Sunday did not guarantee that if Sunday opening became widespread the number of volunteers would expand to fit the demand – especially when shops were given the power, as they would be under the new Wages Bill, to reduce the premiums on Sunday labour in order to balance their books. And secondly, as the Auld Committee reported, the House of Fraser, which opened in Scotland for one or two Sundays before Christmas, had 'recently found the numbers of volunteers diminishing despite the relatively high pay levels.' In short, it looked as though the only reliable safeguard for the shopworker's freedom of choice was some form of restriction of opening hours.

But the repeal of the Shops Act 1950 held a second danger for shop employees. Although they made up one-eleventh of the working population, they were not an advantaged group. For the most part they lacked trade union protection and were poorly paid; male shopworkers earned a little more than a third of the national average for men and the female shopworkers a little more than half of the national average for women. The upshot was that many of them could easily be exploited through low wage levels and intolerable conditions of work.

Until now their legal protection had come from two main sources – Part II of the Shops Act, and the Wages Councils. The Wages Councils were the more crucial; they provided protection for 2.7 million of the country's lowest paid workers, laying down minimum pay levels, rates of pay for overtime, weekends and bank holiday working, as well as minimum holiday requirements. The Shops Act protected shop employees in two ways; one, it limited the hours they could be made to work by guaranteeing most shops would be closed on Sunday; and two, it indirectly kept wage levels buoyant by preventing a slide into greater part-time working which seemed likely to occur if shops were open seven days a week.

The Government seemed almost certain to abolish the Shops Act legislation on the grounds that it was too rigid for modern conditions, and that anyway those provisions referring to young people were duplicated in other legislation. (This was only partly true. Nowhere in existing legislation were there limitations on the number of Sundays a young person could be employed, or the number of weeks in which an employer could engage him or her for overtime work.) But the greater problem was that in the new Wages Bill Ministers were planning to abolish the Wages Councils. This was in the interests of reducing unemployment – a statutory floor on wage levels, they believed, limited the number of people who could be employed, and so kept people out of work. Faced with the resulting depressive effect on wages most other employment groups could protect themselves by reaching a collective agreement with the employer through their union. But this was not true of many shopworkers, the majority of whom were not members of USDAW. Thus for the Government to take away not only the statutory protection against long hours of work, but also the body that guaranteed a minimum wage and premium payments for unsocial hours and overtime, was to the shopworkers a devastating blow.

The unpopularity of this twin offensive even in Parliamentary circles was indicated by the fact that both the Auld Committee and the House of Commons Select Committee on Employment had come out strongly in favour of retaining Wages Councils. The Auld Report, which also recommended that Wages Councils be backed up by an adequately staffed Inspectorate to enforce their Orders, spelt out the consequence of abolition:

. . .there would be a strong likelihood of exploitation of some shopworkers in the form of lower wages, particularly for unsociable hours of work, and possibly in a longer working week. No doubt most good employers would continue to pay the established rates, but in the rapidly changing and uncertain conditions that might follow de-regulation of shop opening hours, if our recommendations were to be adopted, we cannot be sure that all employers would do so.

The high risk of damage to shopworkers and the family if the Government implemented the Auld Report's main conclusion was more than enough to justify opposition to a new Shops Bill. But in addition it was apparent that Sunday trading would have a number of undesirable knock-on effects.

The Auld Committee had acknowledged that 'longer opening hours would be likely to lead to some acceleration of the trend towards the disappearance from the market place

44

of independent traders. . .' The independent traders themselves knew this; in a survey carried out in the spring of that year the Association of Independent Retailers had found that eighty-three percent were opposed to the removal of all restrictions, and sixty-two percent thought the present restrictions should stay. From the standpoint of the free market, of course, the demise of the small trader was inevitable, even necessary; but that kind of economic theory did not take account of the role played by small, local shops. Many people used them for 'topping up' purchases of perishable goods and would be inconvenienced by their loss. Others – the infirm, the immobile, and large numbers of elderly pensioners – depended on them and would find a longer trip to a supermarket a positive hardship. In a survey of corner shops in Cambridge the Jubilee Centre discovered that nearly a third of their customers were elderly or disabled.

Secondly there was no doubt that the deregulation of Sunday trading would drastically change the quality of Sunday. The Bishop of Southwark put it like this:

> How many of those who voted in favour of total deregulation actually live in the cities at weekends and close to large shopping areas? How many of them would have to go to work themselves? If you live in the country, a few shops opening in your village or local town may make little or no difference. But a repetition of Saturday in Streatham High Road (where I live) is a different matter. More traffic, more off street parking, more noise and fumes, more accident and police services, local churchgoers unable to park near their church – the list is a long one.
>
> *The House Magazine,* 7th February 1986

The jibe at the businessmen and legislators to whom Sunday trading caused no personal inconvenience was picked up again at a later date by a writer to the *Sunday Telegraph:*

> Sir,
> It would be a pleasant gesture if the Commons met one Sunday morning to complete the work on the Shops Act.

For a Bishop to place churchgoers among the victims of a new Shops Bill inevitably invited comments of the 'Well, he would say that, wouldn't he?' variety. But the Bishop of Southwark was right to do so. Figures in HMSO publication *Social Trends* estimated that in 1985 Britain had 7.3 million adult church members; moreover a poll conducted by the Bible Society two years earlier had revealed the surprising fact that eighty-four percent of people in England considered themselves affiliated to a Christian church. In anybody's language churchgoers were a significant interest group. And it was clear that unrestricted Sunday trading would have ramifications for them; the more jobs needed to be done on a Sunday, the greater the extent to which congregations would be fragmented; the more commercial activity took place on a Sunday, the more outside noise would disturb worship in characteristically old and inadequately soundproofed buildings; the less the public consciousness of Sunday as a special day, the more numerous the obstacles to new believers finding and building up a faith. None of these, of course, justified the church in imposing its wishes on a largely unbelieveing public, but they were sound reasons for the church to fight its corner on the same basis as any other social group threatened by the effects of deregulation.

Why Keep Sunday Special was published and released at a modest dinner party at a London hotel in July 1985. This was a milestone not so much because we now had a comprehensive and well-documented reply to the Auld Report (although that was important) but because it gave the campaign – now named the Keep Sunday Special Information Campaign – a measure of public profile.

It also drew attention to the fact that opposing new shops legislation was more than simply a church initiative. Of course it was uniting the Christian denominations, within and without, in a quite spectacular fashion (as the Bishop of Birmingham commented later, 'It takes a very great deal to unite the Church of England in this way, but this Bill has achieved it'). But there were other groups – political, trades union and commercial – who had fought deregulation before and were now lining up with the churches to form a broad front of opposition to the Auld Report and to any legislation drafted on its recommendations. This so-called 'unholy alliance' had seen off more than a dozen attempts in the last decade to introduce deregulation through Private Member's Bills. Now, though, the challenge was stronger; the opponents of Sunday trading faced, not a Private Member's Bill, but a Government possessing both the will and the means to drive their legislation through.

This time the unholy alliance wasn't enough.

Chapter 4

Begging to Differ

Talks with the NCT/The Keep Sunday Special Coalition/How to Tidy up the Law/The Queen's Speech/The Bill goes to the Lords/Meaning of the three-line whip/Ivor Stanbrook and the Conservative rebellion/Lord Graham/Tactics in the Lords.

Almost the first action I took when I returned from Africa after the noting of the Auld Report was to write to Leslie Seeney, Director General of the National Chamber of Trade.

The NCT was a confederation of local Chambers of Trade and specific trade associations which in total represented around 200,000 small businesses spread throughout the United Kingdom. As an estimated eighty percent of these businesses had retailing interests, and the policies of the NCT were developed in consultation with the membership at large, it was hardly surprising that until 1980 the Chamber's official line on Sunday trading – affirmed at several conferences and referendums – was that there should be no extension whatever beyond the provisions of the 1950 Act. It was only growing pressure from the large DIY multiples for repeal of the Shops Act which persuaded the NCT's Board of Management that some form of compromise might be the most effective protection for their membership. Still, they were vigorously opposed to total deregulation, and had for some time carried out extensive lobbying of Members of both Houses of Parliament.

I told Leslie Seeney that the Jubilee Centre was entering the dispute and asked if he would be interested in representing the NCT at a meeting convened to develop positive legal alternatives to deregulation based on a tidying-up of the existing Shops Act. Of course joint action was a possibility

48

the NCT had already considered. The problem was one of precedence; a united front would obviously be more effective than a series of individual lobbies, but even though the National Chamber of Trade, USDAW, and the Co-operative Union were all large enough to provide the complex logistical framework necessary for a mass campaign, none would willingly come under another's name. For that reason, although consultations had taken place some time previously between the NCT and USDAW, the two organisations had agreed only to exchange confidences and were not working in harness.

In this respect the arrival of the Jubilee Cetre was very opportune. We had no status, no reputation to keep up, not even a formal affiliation with the church for which we claimed to speak. Consequently, in spite of the fact that in comparison to bodies like the NCT, we were incredibly unsophisticated, our offer to administrate meetings of the kind I outlined to Leslie Seeney was widely accepted by the various groups opposing the new Government legislation. That didn't mean that every group invited to the first meeting of what became the Keep Sunday Special Coalition actually agreed to participate. The John Lewis Partnership, for instance, was already fighting an effective campaign of its own and preferred to pursue its own course. And while John Flood, the Deputy General Secretary of USDAW, was both helpful and co-operative, his union conference had already decided not to take part in a multilateral initiative.

Nonetheless the representation on the afternoon of 26th June was broadbased; the NCT was there, along with a number of its affiliate associations; also the Co-operative Union, the Church of England, the British Council of Churches and – last but not least – Cambridge City Council's Environmental Health Department. This meeting, like all that followed, convened at Maltravers Street in London under the Chairmanship of Viscount Brentford, an experienced solicitor and Parliamentary opponent of Sunday trading.

Our aim to co-operate as fully as possible on the basis of our common hostility to the idea of total deregulation was implemented immediately with decisions to invite in other groups (notably the Roman Catholic Church and, on Leslie

49

Seeney's advice, the British Hardware Federation), and to seek endorsement from our respective executive councils for a combined poster and leaflet campaign in the autumn. We were aware, however, that this was a reactionary stance. After all, no one pretended that the existing Shops Act was satisfactory; that was why the Auld Report had been commissioned in the first place. So if we planned to shout down the Auld Committee's proposals the onus was on us to come up with something better. As its first objective, therefore, the committee agreed to develop and publish an alternative to total deregulation.

It was a task beset with problems.

This wasn't owing to a lack of sensible compromises over Sunday trading; but rather because it was virtually impossible to find one that protected everybody's interests simultaneously. Members of the National Federation of Meat Traders, for example, were so threatened by encroachments on their market that in the 1950 Act they had demanded the inclusion of a clause specifically banning the sale of meat on Sunday, and they were adamant that a similar prohibition be included in new legislation. Consequently, finding common ground acceptable to everyone was arduous and time-consuming, and produced some frank exchanges of opinion.

At the second meeting a subcommittee was set up to consider the two main sets of proposals – one from the Jubilee Centre, the other an alternative Bill drafted on a contingency basis by the NCT in 1981 – and the resulting document was circulated and revised. The measure it put forward centred on a revised list of goods exempt from the Sunday ban, and a new definition of the times and places from which certain items could be sold. Even so, when the final version was discussed by the Keep Sunday Special Coalition on 11th October, the Co-op felt unable to back it, and the Roman Catholic and Church of England representatives made it clear that their denominations could not back any proposals at all. But we had to make some sort of recommendation, so the revised document was published under the title *Sunday Trading: How To Tidy Up The Law*, and launched at the Press Centre in London on 7th October.

Over the summer the Jubilee Centre continued to work

extraordinary hours to extend its constituency support. I had already taken the difficult decision to reduce our family holiday to a week; but even so it wasn't safe from intrusion, and in seven days I spoke at three separate church meetings, in Exeter, Taunton and Southampton. During September the Jubilee Centre ran a weekend conference in Reading for the constituency co-ordinators. Our initial reaction was one of disappointment; only thirty-seven attended, and with one or two notable exceptions, such as Alec Frame, experience of political campaigning was spread pretty thin. But one quality they did all possess – intense commitment; so much so that by the end of the conference I knew it had been a turning point. People like Michael Taylor from Bolton and Geoffrey Fogwill from Cheltenham went back to their respective regions determined to mount effective local campaigns. And that – with a little support from the Jubilee Centre – was exactly what they went on to do.

Early in the same month an important reshuffle in the Cabinet took place to accommodate Norman Tebbit's transference to chairmanship of the Conservative Party. His place as Secretary of State for Trade and Industry was taken by Leon Brittan, who thus made way for Douglas Hurd to become the new Home Secretary. Douglas Hurd was known to be a churchman, and unlike his predecessor had not been a motive force behind the development of Sunday trading legislation. Whatever his views on the issue, on 6th November, Margaret Thatcher confirmed in the Queen's Speech that 'a Bill will be introduced to remove statutory restrictions on shop opening hours', and suddenly, after the long wait of summer, the pressure was on.

When the wording of the Bill was released it turned out to have three main provisions. One – as expected – the complete deregulation of trading hours both on Sundays and weekdays; two, the abolition of most statutory protection of shopworkers, including mealbreaks; and three, a provision to protect established but not future employees from unfair dismissal if they refused to work on Sundays.

On the day after the Queen's Speech the Catholic Bishops' Conference made a press statement calling on the Government to allow a free vote when the Bill was debated in Parliament.

The Keep Sunday Special Coalition had already written to a range of retail organisations, churches and local authorities, asking them to subscribe to the statement 'We totally oppose the complete deregulation of Sunday trading recommended by the Auld Committee'. 110 replied, among them the John Lewis Partnership, Selfridges, Argos and the Mothers' Union and the communication of this fact to MPs by Viscount Brentford was made public in a second press release on the same day.

These murmurs of dissent by what the *London Standard* called an 'alliance of vested interests . . . threatening to scupper one of the Government's most popular and long-awaited proposals' may possibly have prompted the Home Office to invite a number of leading opponents to discuss the issue with David Waddington MP, the Bill's official sponsor, a few days later. At any rate discussion was abortive; it was clear the Government was intent on pushing the Bill through without amendments, and we could only hope that there would be enough time before it reached its Second Reading in the House of Commons for us to rally some effective opposition. As things stood, time was not on our side.

But there followed a fatal miscalculation by the Government. Had they, as we anticipated, pushed the Shops Bill into the Commons immediately, we would almost certainly have been caught wrong-footed. We simply hadn't had sufficient time to publicise the issues. Consequently, the Government would have been able without much difficulty to win the Second Reading, force the Bill safely in and out of Committee, and take it into the Lords – where, if necessary, they could pull out a couple of hundred Conservative backbenchers to make it law. But they didn't put the Bill into the Commons; instead, probably because the Commons already had a very heavy legislative programme, they took the unusual step of introducing the Bill in the Lords. The First Reading in the Lords was set for Thursday, 14th November, the Second – where the principle of the Bill was voted on would likely follow before the end of the month.

Outside opposition, of course, was of less importance to the Government than opposition within the House, and particularly from the Back Benches of its own party. If the Bill was lost, the cause would be rebellion in the rank and file of Conservative MPs; and although at this stage the danger of losing the Bill was neglible the Government Whips were nonetheless keeping a cautious eye on backbench opinion.

They detected a degree of discontent. Some Conservative MPs, who had felt Cabinet pressure for Shops Act reform through Leon Brittan and Lord Young building up in the early 1980s, wanted to know why the issue had not been mentioned in the Party manifesto. A measure that urged such a profound change in Britain's way of life surely demanded an electoral mandate. In addition, it had angered many of them that in the Auld Report debate in May what was traditionally a conscience issue had been made the subject of a three-line whip. Worse than that, the Government had actually gone back on its word, for before the Auld Committee began its work David Mellor, then Under-Secretary of State for the Home Office, had said in the Commons:

> 'There are important considerations and fears about the character of Sunday. These fears are held in many parts of the House and I agree that they are an important factor. That is why the Government adhere to the view, which successive Governments have adhered to, that the decision must be for the individual conscience of Hon. Members.'

Traditionally, the three-line whip was a device employed by a Parliamentary party needing a full turn out of its MPs to ensure either the safe passage of its own legislation or the maximum chance of defeating legislation put forward by an opposing Government. It exerted a strong social and political pressure on MPs to toe the party line. Failure to comply being viewed as an act of disloyalty, it was usual in the case of an important vote for potential rebels to receive a sticky interview with the Chief Whip. Rebellion would always put your promotion prospects in doubt; if you had achieved a Ministerial or Junior Ministerial post it might force your resignation.

The three-line whip, however, did not extend to Private

53

Members' Bills, and if matters of conscience were raised it was often dropped even if the Bill formed part of the Government's legislative agenda, as occurred in 1981 with the Bill proposing compulsory wearing of seatbelts. A conscience issue was widely regarded as one above the realm of an administration's social or economic policy. Accordingly the abolition of the death penalty had been carried on a free vote in 1938, as had the liberalisation of the abortion law in 1967.

Since Sunday trading had always been treated as a matter of conscience, the decision of the Government to impose a whip was disturbing for two reasons.

Firstly, it made Sunday into a party political issue. In other words, it reduced the debate over the special status of Sunday in British life to a simple competition of interest between rival factions; put crudely, the Government against the 'Sabbatarians'. Obviously all moral issues produced divisions of opinion, abortion and the death penalty included; but in matters of conscience it wasn't only public opinion that counted – there was also an agreement that a thing was 'right' or 'wrong', 'good', or 'bad', in a way quite independent of the degree of support it enjoyed in one or another section of the community. Granted that the democratic political process allowed for people's views on a conscience issue to be expressed through pressure groups and the media, it was (apart from anything else) flying in the face of Parliamentary tradition to approach such an issue purely on the grounds of economic expediency or 'public opinion'. Which suggested a second cause for concern at the Government's use of the whip; for once the precedent had been set with Sunday trading, might it not be used again at some future date, about say, euthanasia?

At any rate, following the Queen's Speech and on the basis of considerations like these, an Early Day Motion was put down in the House of Commons by Ann Winterton, MP, requesting a free vote on the Shops Bill. An Early Day Motion was a means by which MPs could register their objections to a Bill before it came before Parliament, and so provide a measure of the strength of feeling against it. In the same week Ivor Stanbrook, a respected Conservative MP who had voted against the noting of the Auld Report, told the 1922 Committee that he planned to convene a meeting of Conservative Members to discuss possible action over the Government's proposals. The meeting was attended by about a dozen MPs – including Sir Bernard Braine, Kenneth Lewis and Jill Knight, doughty establishment figures on the back bench – who decided that the issue should be kept bubbling in Parliamentary questions, and agreed to refer the media to Ivor Stanbrook as spokesman for the group.

The decision to use Parliamentary questions was adept in view of the large quantity of correspondence the Government was now receiving thanks largely to the ProSunday Coalition. In March of 1985 Leon Brittan had told the House of Commons that since the publication of the Auld Report there had arrived 166 letters in support of its recommendations and 362 against – figures from which he declined to draw any 'significant conclusions'. (In the same exchange Dennis Skinner – not known for his sympathy with the Conservatives – had warned the Home Secretary to beware of an alliance between the unions and the churches, to which Leon Brittan replied: 'I am sure that is an apt warning, and, coming from the quarter that it does, I shall take it in the spirit in which it was intended.') Eight months later, when subsequent to Ivor Stanbrook's meeting, David Waddington gave a parliamentary Written Answer on correspondence received since the publication of the Bill, the figures had changed dramatically: twenty-four in favour, and 6,664 against.

To co-ordinate our strategy for the House of Lords, Viscount Brentford invited Lord Graham to Maltravers Street for the Keep Sunday Special Coalition meeting on 11th November.

A member of the Co-op and USDAW, and an MP for ten years before he received his peerage, Lord Graham had played a major role in the defeat of previous attempts to deregulate Sunday trading. He was therefore a formidable ally. We learned from him that a general strategy for tackling the Shops Bill in the Lords had already been worked out in consultation with Gerald Kaufman (for the Labour front bench) and the

55

Labour MPs sponsored respectively by the Co-op and USDAW. These groups represented a range of opinion, as did the membership of the Coalition; the Co-operative Union, for instance, being an employer, was more firmly opposed to Clause 1 of the Shops Bill (relating to opening hours) than the rest of the Labour movement, which in general laid more stress on Clauses 2 and 3. On the need to defeat the Shops Bill, however, they were in complete unanimity, and their method was simple: *delay*.

'The Second Reading's been put back to 2nd December. After the vote the Bill will be referred to the Committee of the Whole House. The Government have set down two days for the Committee Stage – December 16 and 17 – so they're in a hurry.'

Someone asked if it was worth trying to defeat the Bill at its Second Reading in the Lords.

'No. There's a convention known as the Salisbury Doctrine, which means the House of Lords won't defeat a Bill at Second Reading if it's been put forward by the elected Government. If we tried, we'd only lose our support and tighten the whip. The only thing we can do at Second Reading is to submit a reasoned amendment to register the extent of the opposition.'

He was firm over Parliamentary tactics.

'We delay. The Government wants the Bill out of Committee before Christmas, and out of the Lords by the end of January. What we've got to do is table enough amendments at Committee Stage that we need an extra day to finish it. Under normal circumstances that would give us two, maybe three days. But that late in the session there won't be room to schedule another Committee day until the New Year. So we gain a month, and keep the Bill in the Lords until the end of February.'

'There's no chance of denting the Bill with an amendment?'

'Possibly. But remember that amendments made in Committee can be overturned at the Report Stage. What we're really winning here is time.'

He was right. The question was; how could we put it to best use?

Chapter 5

Strategy

*Michael Windridge/The birth of the Keep Sunday Special Campaign/
Guiding Principles/Opinion and opinion polls/Campaign strategy/The
Bill in the Lords/Northern Ireland*

More than once over the last six months I had expressed
the view that we needed advice on our public relations. The
idea had never received unanimous approval, partly because
the hiring of a PR firm went way beyond the Coalition's
limited finances. A couple of days after the Queen's Speech,
however, I received a telephone call from Michael Windridge,
a publicity consultant, who said he was interested in the issue
of Sunday trading and would like to sit in at one of our
meetings. I told him to come along on 11th November which
he did. He called me at the Jubilee Centre the next morning.

'I think you ought to form a campaign.'

'Do we have time?'

'If Lord Graham meant what he said last night. But you'll
have to make an impact on public opinion to get any chance
of winning this one.'

'Okay,' I said. 'What about giving us some advice?'

'Well I'd be prepared to do that, but either I'll have to do
it in the evenings, or you'll have to employ me.'

'How much?'

'You'll need an initial payment of £10,000. After that we
could discuss some options.'

I put the phone down, biting my lip. We were talking
about a lot of money – money that at this moment we simply
didn't have. On the other hand Keep Sunday Special was
supported directly or indirectly by some large organisations,
and Michael Windridge was a very able man whose skills

we badly needed. I hesitated, then took the plunge. The following week I urged acceptance of the offer, and when the meeting was over asked the representatives of the key member groups to stay behind.

'We can only have this help if we're willing to pay for it. So I want to go around the table now and find out how much our executives are willing to pledge.'

Each person named a figure. To my great surprise the total topped £8,000. There was no argument, no wrangling. Everyone wanted to make the downpayment and get the campaign underway. At the next meeting plans were approved to retain a consultancy from Michael Windridge's firm Extel for a period of four months; invitations were sent to possible patrons, and a working basis for the Keep Sunday Special Campaign was drawn up between the founder members; the British Council of Churches, the British Hardware Federation, the Multiple Shoe Retailers Association, the National Federation of Meat Traders, the National Chamber of Trade and the Jubilee Centre.

Michael's arrival brought abrupt changes in the structure of the old Coalition. From now on the group meeting at Maltravers Street became the Steering Committee; but although most initiatives were discussed at the now weekly meetings the day to day running of the campaign was left to Michael Windridge and me. It had to be; there simply wasn't time to get every decision approved before we took it. So the movement arranged itself into a sort of pyramid. The executive partnership at the top rested on a large group of people representing allied or member organisations, and this in turn rested on a constituency network covering much of the country and held together by the Jubilee Centre.

Almost at once we laid down two guiding principles. The first was a drastic simplification of goals. Until now there had been differing views on what a campaign might seek to achieve; certainly at the beginning of the summer the Jubilee Centre had been inclined to see the Sunday battle as an opportunity for evangelism as well as a fight for social justice. But Michael was adamant that we set our sights on a single target. In the words of Extel's outline proposal: 'The overriding objective of the Campaign is to secure the withdrawal or substantial amendment of the Shops Bill (Lords) 1985'.

The second guiding principle was an almost obsessive concern for strategy.

In outline this was fairly straightforward – we tried to embarrass the Government by showing that the Shops Bill did not have the support of the British public. Seven day trading, after all, was not only missing from the last Conservative Manifesto but in actual fact a contradiction of it. The stated ideals of the Government were 'to defend Britain's traditional liberties and distinctive way of life' and 'to build a responsible society which protects the weak but also allows the family and the individual to flourish'. The conspicuous failure of the Shops Bill to do any of these things may not have been a deliberate act of deceit so much as a piece of muddled thinking: in the words of the Bishop of Southwark, 'the clash between a principle about economic freedom and a principle about conserving stable values' (*House Magazine*, 7th February 1986). In short, if devotion to the free market and the defence of British tradition sat at opposite ends of a legislative see-saw, the Shops Bill was legitimate only on the basis of some intellectual jiggery-pokery that pretended both ends could be on the ground at the same time.

Informing the electorate of what was being done to their mandate was therefore an important cornerstone of the Campaign's strategy. But of course the Government and the various supporters of deregulation could always sidestep the accusation by claiming that – regardless of the promises made or not made at the last election – the British public clearly wanted the freedom to shop on Sundays. Leon Brittan had said as much to Gerald Kaufman in the debate on the Auld Report when he described the present law as 'unacceptable because it is no longer one that the majority of people want'.

This argument had been given extensive airing in the media. But if you put on one side the obvious objection – that a law could be right even when it was unpopular – it remained to be shown that 'the majority of people' did in fact want Sunday trading, and to this end voluminous proof had been amassed through the use of opinion polls. To take a fairly typical example, when asked in a MORI poll in 1983 whether they thought 'that the law should be changed to allow shops to open on Sundays . .' Sixty-five percent of respondents agreed that it should. From results like this, which were quoted copiously the conclusion was drawn again and again that customers wanted Sunday trading.

But there were immense problems with this kind of survey. For one thing it was generally assumed that the person responding already had an opinion on the subject and was not making an instantaneous judgement on the basis of information supplied with the question or the phrasing of the question itself. It was obvious that if you asked somebody whether he wanted the 'freedom to shop on Sundays' he was apt to say yes – until you reminded him that Sunday trading could increase street noise and put up the price of his groceries. But whether he said yes or no the chances were that he had never really bothered to work out the implications in a way that would recommend his opinion as an 'informed one'. And if the majority of your respondents were like that, your opinion poll would be little more than a survey of snap judgements.

One consequence of this was that taken together polls often showed the public to want contradictory things. Most people will say that – all other things being equal – they would like the convenience of being able to shop when they want. At the same time, the National Consumer Council, in correspondence with the Auld Committee, said that 'there is a general desire that Sunday should be a "different" day', and the Auld Report noted that respondents to NCC surveys 'felt very strongly that staff should not be forced to work on Sundays'. Starting from Leon Brittan's premise that the law should be changed to accommodate public opinion, it was extremely hard to see how changes could be made that satisfied both demands. You might as well have approached the public with the question 'Would you like everything to be better for everybody?' and then gone to Westminster with a resounding yes to see what MPs were going to do about it.

Quite apart from this, however, close scrutiny of the actual results of opinion polls revealed that the demand for Sunday opening only extended across a narrow band of the retail trade. Another MORI poll, conducted for the IFS in 1984, had asked respondents which of a range of products they would 'be likely to buy at least occasionally on a Sunday'. Forty percent said DIY/decorating materials, thirty-eight said garden products. After that the next four categories of goods registered scores between twelve and twenty-one percent; the rest managed only single figure percentages. Furthermore, according to the Auld Report a 1981 study by the NCC 'into the problems that people face in doing their shopping. . . found that just one in ten respondents said they found existing shopping hours inconvenient.' In fact, 'the goods which people suggest they would like to buy on Sunday are, in the main, those which are already available on Sundays.' This did not argue for extensive changes in the law, and it was significant that the Auld Committee summed up: 'It would be misleading. . . to leave the impression that there is an incessant general clamour for Sunday shopping or longer trading hours'.

We knew there was a strong possibility these views would alter with time. After all, most of the people who commissioned these opinion polls were less concerned about measuring public opinion than changing it. If there really was an identifiable majority view on Sunday trading, that view was not static; it could be turned even by the insistence of influential people that it was already facing in another direction. Consequently it was of utmost importance, firstly to make sure people were clearly informed on the issues surrounding Sunday trading, and secondly, to create devices capable of demonstrating to MPs and public alike that support for the Shops Bill was dangerously thin.

Strategy. Nothing was more important. I carved out whole mornings and afternoons from an incredibly busy schedule of engagements and correspondence just to sit at the Extel offices and sift ideas. Usually I was with Michael Windridge, sometimes also with Michael McNair-Wilson, a backbench Conservative MP and director of Extel whose seventeen years in Parliament had given him an outstanding grasp of the subtleties of procedure and lobbying. It could take us three hours just to ensure some detail of wording was correct, or schedule an event to peak at the right moment, or rule out an option that looked attractive but would eat up precious man-hours for almost no result. Every major feature had to be checked over laboriously in case of flaws; weighed, chipped into shape, worn smooth under pressure of repeated examination.

So, gradually, the outlines of the campaign emerged. The letter writing was well under way by this time; but in addition to this we planned three further initiatives. First, an official launch was needed to make the Campaign's presence felt in the national media. Eventually we decided to stage this on 9th January midway between the Christmas lull and the start of the new Parliamentary session on 13th January, being in the middle of the week that would also allow the Sunday papers to get hold of the story. This was to be followed by an opinion poll and a nationwide petition. We had few doubts over the opinion poll – it simply had to be shown that when you asked fair questions you did not end up showing massive and bogus majorities in favour of Sunday trading – but we argued almost interminably over the petition. Could it be completed in time? Would we get enough signatures? Eventually Michael brought us down to bottom line; if we wanted to win, we couldn't afford not to canvass support with a petition. USDAW had told us they planned to raise one among the shopworkers, and it seemed possible that by the time the Shops Bill reached its Second Reading in the House of Commons USDAW and the churches between them might collect half a million signatures – enough, at least, to make a noise when the bundle landed on the Government's doorstep.

The final and most important initiative depended heavily on the Jubilee Centre's ability to organise its grassroots network. We wanted to arrange constituency meetings. As many as possible. The meetings would be widely advertised, and the local MP, perhaps along with some local personalities, invited to speak and answer questions on the Sunday issue. If, as we hoped, local Christians were willing to turn out in force, MPs would get first hand experience of the opposition the Shops Bill was stirring up among the voters. The intention was not to drub a Member of Parliament into submission to the Campaign's perspective on Sunday trading, but to show the strength of the argument against deregulation and the extent of the support such an argument enjoyed in the electorate. Three hundred meetings like that, we felt, perhaps followed up by a mass rally in Central London, would do more than anything else to stress at Westminster the political riskiness of the Shops Bill.

The timing of these meetings was crucial. If we waited until after the Bill's Second Reading in the Commons its supporters would be able to argue that since the Bill had already been approved in principle, there was little reason to tinker with it in Committee. (Indeed, since in the Commons – though not in the Lords – the Committee constituted not the whole House, but a group of around twenty-four MPs whose membership reflected the Government's overall majority, winning an amendment could prove extremely difficult.) Not only that – we didn't even know when the Second Reading was going to be. Because the Jubilee Centre was struggling to complete its constituency network we needed as much time as we could get to prepare the meetings. But we couldn't push the date back too far – there was always a chance we wouldn't be able to hold the Bill in the Lords, and if it suddenly came out and the Government brought forward the Second Reading in the Commons we'd be left high and dry.

We sought Lord Graham's advice.

'If they really rammed it through it's possible the Government could have the Bill in the Commons by 18th February.'

'Is that likely?'

'If we're very unlucky'

'What do you think?' I said, looking at Michael Windridge. 'Should we chance it?'

But he shook his head. 'No. No risks. We'll take the last Friday before that date, and give it our best shot.'

So the constituency meetings were scheduled for Friday, 14th February.

We dubbed the plan Operation Valentine.

As expected, the Shops Bill received its First Reading in the Lords on 14th November.

The following day an event occurred which, though it seemed at the time to draw attention away from the Sunday trading dispute, was ultimately of enormous relevance to it.

On their third formal bilateral meeting the Prime Minister Margaret Thatcher and the Irish *Taoiseach* Dr Garret FitzGerald signed the Anglo-Irish Agreement.

The move was immediately denounced by both main Unionist parties in Northern Ireland, the Official Unionist Party (OUP) and the Democratic Unionist Party (DUP), which held eleven and three respectively of the fifteen Northern Irish seats at Westminster, the fifteenth belonging to James Kilfedder of the Ulster Popular Unionist Party.

Loyalist anger was soon given vent in the Belfast rally on Sunday 24th November where between 50,000 and 100,000 protestors heard all the Unionist MPs except one – Enoch Powell – pledge to resign their seats. Nonetheless in the following week the Anglo-Irish Agreement was given official approval in Parliament, first by the Lords on 26th November and a day later by the Commons. The Commons vote was carried 473:47, twenty Conservative MPs going against the Government. Ian Gow, who until his resignation over the Government's Northern Ireland policy was Minister of State at the Treasury and widely regarded as one of Mrs Thatcher's most consistent supporters, warned that the move would 'prolong and . . .not diminish Ulster's agony.' After the vote Ian Paisley and the OUP deputy leader Peter Robinson immediately tendered their resignations as MPs by the traditional method of applying for stewardship of the Chiltern Hundreds and the Manor of Northstead. The other thirteen Unionist MPs followed, including Enoch Powell.

The Lord's Second Reading of the Shops Bill came up on the Monday of the following week, 2nd December. In accordance with Lord Graham's advice a reasoned amendment had been tabled by Hugh Montefiore, the Bishop of Birmingham. The purpose of a reasoned amendment at Second Reading was not to declare outright opposition to a Bill, but to put forward a specific reason why it should not be considered in its present form. The Bishop's amendment in this case moved that the Bill be read a second time but with the rider that 'this House considers the law should be amended so as to rationalise restrictions on trading hours without such extensive deregulation as the Bill proposes'.

As it happened, the bishops themselves became something

of a target during the debate. In part this reflected the Government's frustration that the churches had fallen in with such unanimity behind the Sunday cause; it may also have had something to do with the Church of England's report *Faith In the City*, a trenchant critique of Conservative policy in the inner cities, which was being strongly attacked by Government spokesmen even though its launch still wasn't due for another twenty-four hours. At any rate, in her summing up for the Government Baroness Trumpington had no qualms about airing the ecclesiastical laundry. Having cited a number of the Lord Bishops' dioceses she concluded:

'. . .if any of your Lordships should happen to visit Birmingham Cathedral on a Sunday you would find its excellent church shop open from 11am to 3pm, selling church literature and various souvenirs, including key rings, pens, cards, books, diaries, and so on. I hope I shall not be struck by a fiery bolt if I say that as the law stands the deans and chapters of these cathedrals are guilty of criminal offences in being open for the sale of these objects. . .'

The other matter dwelt on by the Lords in favour of the Bill was the inadequacy of any existing compromise solution. Lord Simon devoted several minutes to disparaging the Keep Sunday Special Coalition's document *How To Tidy Up The Law*. After more than nine hours of debate, in the distinctive language of Parliament the amendment was 'disagreed to' and the Bill referred to the Committee of the Whole House.

Now what Lord Graham called the 'trench warfare' of the Committee Stage began. Two conventions governed legislative procedure in the Lords; one was that however many amendments you tabled, they were divided into two equal groups and each group assigned a day; the other was that the business of the House concluded at or shortly after 10.30pm. So the greater the number of amendments and the greater the number of people speaking to each amendment, the less likely it was that the Committee Stage could be completed in two days. Of course the House could remain sitting into the early hours if necessary, but if an amendment was voted down at 1am with fewer than thirty Members in attendance the House would fall along with the amendment and another day's Committee work would be unavoidable.

Lord Graham had co-ordinated more than forty amendments to the Shops Bill. By 11.02pm on the first Committee day, 16th December, only ten of them had been considered. The total had risen to thirteen by the end of the next day's sitting, which left about thirty amendments still to be voted on. As Lord Graham had predicted, the next Committee day had to be scheduled for January. On Friday 20th December Parliament rose for the Christmas Recess.

Chapter 6

A Revolt in the Upper House

Moving house/The launch and the Westland crisis/Support from Scotland/Planning Operation Valentine/The Co-op survey/Problems for the Government/Problems for the Campaign/Clive Ponting/The Denning Amendment.

Between Christmas and New Year I managed a flying visit to Scotland. I was concerned that the Scottish example was being cited so often by the opposition to show the limited effect of seven day trading on the character of Sunday. The story I got from church leaders in Glasgow and Edinburgh was different; they expressed deep misgivings about the steady increase in Sunday opening north of the border, and agreed to seek support against the Bill from retailers and shopworkers – a decision which later bore fruit in a Scottish press conference.

At the Jubilee Centre, meanwhile, things were close to chaos.

Under Alasdair's management we had been taking on large numbers of extra staff. He had employed a personal assistant in the form of Martin Graham, a graduate in political theory and government, whose expertise was already being put to good use in the writing of a booklet on the conscience issue. This was eventually published as *Jubilee Centre Paper No. 6.* early in the New Year, and circulated widely among MPs. But even when Martin went to London as a contact with Extel, that still left seventeen people working in the house at Hangman's Corner. My wife was at her wits' end; the dispatch staff crammed into the eight by sixteen garage were working in scarves and anoraks; and we simply had nowhere to put either the booklets we'd produced or the increasing quantities of mail coming in from our supporters.

With constant urging from Michael Windridge to expand our operation, finding larger premises became an absolute necessity. One large old house had already been turned down on the grounds of inadequate security. By December we had found another building, a three-storey detached house set among rows of tiny terraces near the Cambridge railyards. Although the renovation would take six months, the builder – who lived a mere fifty yards from the site – offered us a cheap rental on some of his own spare office space, and so we took it. The interim accommodation would have been worse than its predecessor had we not been able to rent a second and eventually a third office in the building next door. As it was, the main problem turned out to be one of communication; few of our contacts and correspondents realised that for the duration of the campaign the Jubilee Centre consisted of three chilly rooms served by a desperately overcomplicated system of telephones.

Our working methods were rudimentary, to say the least. There was no time to train incoming staff or even to make sensible demarcations of labour. The work demanded complete flexibility, willingness to put in extra hours and a good measure of tolerance and humour. We had one press list, one Commons list, one Lords list; and one list of constituency co-ordinators – the key to the entire enterprise – which had never grown fast enough over the summer and with the onset of Christmas was still only creeping towards 200.

Against this often frenetic background plans had to be laid for the Campaign's press launch. What we finally came up with looked sure to attract publicity. To illustrate the point that Britain's traditional Sunday was about to be given the carve-up we arranged for everyone at the press conference to receive a joint of beef. Similar joints would be sent to all Cabinet Ministers and an especially large one delivered in a 1930s butcher's van to No. 10 Downing Street. At the same time the President of the Mothers' Union, Hazel Treadgold, would release balloons bearing the Campaign logo in front of Big Ben. Several of the Campaign's patrons had agreed to speak at the launch, including Sir Bernard Braine, the

Bishop of Birmingham, Lord Graham, and Viscount Brentford. Messages of support had been received from all three main church leaders – Archbiship Runcie, Cardinal Hume and the Moderator of the Free Church Council – and these, along with a longer statement from USDAW that supported '100 percent the aims and objectives of the Campaign', were reproduced in the press pack.

All in all, we thought, the launch couldn't fail to get extensive coverage in the national media.

We were mistaken.

The Christmas period was dominated by two major news stories, both of which were to have an important bearing on the fight against the Shops Bill.

Firstly, in two separate incidents at Rome and Vienna Airports on 27th December, sixteen people were killed by terrorist gunmen. Responsibility for the killings was generally attributed to the Palestinian Abu Nidal group, backed by Libya, and as a result the United States imposed economic sanctions on Libya and threatened to make a show of force off the Libyan coast in order to deter Colonel Qaddafi from supporting further acts of terrorism.

The second story had been on the boil for several months already. In June 1985 the Government had agreed that the Bank of England should bring together the main creditors of the ailing Westland Helicopter Company and develop a recovery plan. This led to negotiations with two groups; the United Technology Corporation (UTC), the parent company of the USA's largest helicopter manufacturer, Sikorski; and a European consortium based in West Germany, France and Italy, and later drawing in British Aerospace. The respective merits of the offers made by the two groups were disputed. The Westland board of directors clearly favoured the American package; the Defence Secretary, Michael Heseltine, preferred the European.

Officially the Government was neutral: as Leon Brittan told the Commons on 16th December in his new capacity as Secretary of State for Trade and Industry, 'As a private sector company, it is for Westland to decide the best route to follow to secure its future and that of its employees'. In the New

Year, however, a sequence of events put the Government's neutralilty in question. On 3rd January Michael Heseltine made public a letter to David Horne, the managing director of Lloyds Merchant Bank, financial advisor to the European consortium, confirming that Westland's acceptance of what was now a combined Sikorski/Fiat deal would be 'incompatible' with Westland's participation in some future European defence projects. In response the Solicitor General, Sir Patrick Mayhew, wrote to Michael Heseltine pointing out that his letter implied this problem of 'incompatibility' to have been raised with the British Government by all the European countries involved in the cited defence projects. As this was not the case, the Solicitor General requested that the Defence Secretary write again to David Horne to set the record straight.

Mayhew's letter was leaked. As a result Michael Heseltine felt that the Government, far from being neutral, actively favoured the Sikorski deal, and he resigned, giving as he did so a lengthy press statement. Among other things he accused Leon Brittan of intervention against the European partnership, and suggested that the leaking of Patrick Mayhew's letter had been a deliberate attempt on the part of the Government to discredit his own views on the issue.

By an extraordinary coincidence Michael Heseltine was announcing his resignation on the steps of No. 10 Downing Street almost at the same moment I was at the press conference launching the Keep Sunday Special Campaign. Consequently, none of the national dailies carried our story the next morning, and the Campaign's media coverage was all but stifled. It was true that we were widely reported in the local press, and that I spoke twice on Radio 4 and Sir Bernard Braine made an appearance on breakfast television. But at the Steering Committee meeting on 10th January there was a pervasive feeling that the launch had gone off at halfcock. The Westland affair had even forestalled the Prime Minister's delivery of meat!

After so many hours of meticulous preparation the failure came as a crushing disappointment. Ironically, in the long run it may have been to our advantage – after all a Campaign whose launch made such a feeble impact on the press was unlikely to seem dangerous to its opponents, and so perhaps gave them a false sense of security. But this was not apparent to us at the time. We felt it was vital now to follow up all other initiatives, and accordingly made plans to launch the Campaign separately in Wales and Scotland. Owing to a difference between English and Scots law Scotland already had seven day trading; however it was naive to suppose that this made Scotland immune to the effects of deregulation in England and Wales. The fact was that many of the national multiples like Marks and Spencer remained closed on Sunday in Scotland only because the loss of market share suffered by the small proportion of their stores north of the border had a negligible effect on their overall sales figures. If competition forced them to open in the rest of the country, however, it was extremly doubtful whether they would stay closed in Scotland, and this would quickly push up Scotland's present sixteen percent Sunday opening figures.

Aware of this, the Church of Scotland's Church and Nation Committee met on 16th January and endorsed the Keep Sunday Special Campaign. This was noted at our Steering Committee meeting the following day, as was the willingness of the Roman Catholic Church and USDAW to participate in a Scottish press conference. As it happened, plans were already afoot at the Jubilee Centre to produce a booklet specifically on the effects of deregulation in Scotland, and there was a possibility that the publication of this might be timed to coincide with the launch of a Scottish Keep Sunday Special Campaign.

I kept up a demanding programme of speaking engagements around the country, and corresponded with the management of large retail concerns in an attempt to make known the social and economic costs of deregulation. Understandably many of the leading retailers wanted to keep their options open on Sunday trading. I knew from private conversations with managing directors that the majority preferred to stay closed on Sunday; the problem was, if seven day trading became law and competition forced them into the market place, they didn't want to be seen reneging on public commitment. Persuading them to back press statements proving a strong groundswell of opinion against the Bill therefore became increasingly hard as the campaign progressed.

Perhaps the most important to the Campaign's strategy from now on was Operation Valentine.

Responsibility for implementing this had been delegated chiefly to Tim Law. The aim was to hold meetings in as many constituencies as possible, and since local meetings could never be arranged centrally this meant finding a person in each constituency willing to do the job for that area. By Christmas we had two relevant lists, one of churches, the other of constituency co-ordinators recruited by the churches. So far these co-ordinators had acted as local reps for the Campaign, supplying people with Campaign literature, encouraging them to ask questions at MP's constituency surgeries and, most important, to write to their local MP calling on him or her to oppose the Bill. This had been going on long enough for us to know which co-ordinators were the more motivated, and at the start of 1986 we invited these to take on the additional task of regional co-ordination – in other words, overseeing a group of constituencies and finding a meeting organiser for each.

With the launch in mind Michael Windridge had asked Tim to finalise as many meetings as he could by January. But this hadn't happened, for several reasons. For one thing, regional co-ordinators were another link in the chain of command, and this slowed down communication considerably. Also, Tim himself was being overworked. We solved this by transferring Michael Andreyev, one of the researchers, over to the Jubilee Centre's Campaign department; but that made no difference to the main bottleneck. It didn't matter how efficiently you sent out your material; over the Christmas period very few people were going to respond. Consequently by 9th January the number of confirmed meetings was pitifully small.

So Operation Valentine turned into a race against time. We knew that the success of the Keep Sunday Special Campaign depended entirely on the willingness of local people to make their own views known. There had to be lots of letters; there had to be numerous, well-attended constituency meetings. Without that, no amount of co-operation between the unions and the retailers and the Parliamentary supporters would be able to break down the Government's formidable majority in the Commons. The whole Campaign was carried by people.

At the same time it was the slender but essential function of the Campaign to motivate and inform the public. And so at the beginning of January we began the colossal task of mailing every church on our lists to publicise Operation Valentine. Leaflets, valentine cards, even balloons all had to be packaged and sent off. For an organisation the size of the Jubilee Centre the mailing was a logistical nightmare; there were nearly 10,000 addresses on the Church of England list alone, and after each phase of the mailing the phone lines were jammed for days. We just, and only just, got away with it.

Monday 20th January saw the publication of a survey by Research Bureau Ltd for the Co-operative Union, Britain's biggest retailer. The results were encouraging. Of 150 male and 450 female Co-op customers interviewed at thirty sampling points in England and Wales, only fifteen percent came out in favour of all day Sunday opening, and seventy-two percent said that Sunday opening of shops would make no difference at all to their shopping habits. Significantly, the Co-op study confirmed the conclusions of the MORI poll commissioned by the IFS in 1984, that consumer support for Sunday shopping was selective of particular types of shop; so, for instance, while the majority of respondents were against all shops being open on a Sunday, forty-seven percent were in favour of the opening of DIY stores and garden centres.

'This survey,' commented the Co-op in its press release, 'shows conclusively that the Co-op's opposition to unlimited Sunday trading is closely in line with the views of the majority of our shoppers and shop members.

'Because a market research survey is conducted in greater detail than an opinion poll, and because of the position of the Co-op as Britain's biggest retailer and consumer body, we hope Parliament will take note and act upon these views.'

We were now a week into the new Parliamentary session, and the next day I attended a luncheon put on in the House of Lords by Viscount Brentford to bring together leading Conservative opponents of the Bill. Here for the first time

I met Ivor Stanbrook, the quiet, determined man at the centre of the Conservative rebellion. With him were Sir Bernard Braine, Sir Raymond Gower, and Ann Winterton, originator of the Early Day Motion demanding a free vote on the Second Reading. The success of the letter writing campaign was by now becoming almost embarrassing. In a Commons Written Answer seven days earlier David Waddington had revealed that since the publication of the Shops Bill twenty-seven letters had been received in support of the Bill, and 16,292 against it. Nevertheless, the mood at the luncheon was far from optimistic. The Government was likely to impose a three-line whip in the Commons, and under those conditions, according to Extel's calculation, only thirty more Conservative MPs would oppose the Government at the Second Reading than had voted against the Auld Report. Assuming all of these actually did go into the 'No' lobby we would still need thirty abstentions to come anywhere near defeating the Bill.

In the afternoon Viscount Brentford returned to the Lords for the Bill's third day in Committee. The debates were being followed carefully by the press because the Labour leadership had predicted a close run on an amendment dealing with the protection of shopworkers. It was noticeable that for some earlier amendments concerning the status of Sunday as a 'special' day the bishops turned out in force. But the bishops had left by the time the key amendment – 188 – was presented by Baroness Turner of Camden. This related to Clause 2 of the Bill, and proposed simply that the statutory protection of shopworkers – which the Bill abolished for all those over the age of eighteen – be extended to the retiring age of sixty-five. In the course of a lively debate one of the House's elder Members, the former Prime Minister Harold Macmillan, now the Earl of Stockton, took exception to this proposal. But not on account of its excessive liberality.

'Sixty-five,' he declared, 'is a tuppeny age; a sixty-five year old is quite a young person!'

Several of the noble Lords were heard to rumble, 'Hear, hear!'

Lord Stockton then proceeded to give the Government an unexpected birching.

'What I do not see. . . is the argument that we ought to

go on a quite different issue, a purely economic issue, to this extreme which seems, greatly to my regret, to have inspired part of my party. . .

'The Bill is meant to make it possible for people to trade freely on Sundays. . . that is what the Bill is for. It is not meant to make life more difficult for shop assistants. . .

'Let us remember that the great commandment that was handed down to God's chosen people was perhaps the greatest social reform in the history of civilisation; the concept that every man or woman, however humble, should have at least some period of rest. . .

'If this amendment is not the right method then we should find some other way of enclosing in this Bill a clause that will make it perfectly clear that the Bill does no injury at all, and is prevented from doing any injury at all, to the rights that have been so long-won for the humbler people of our country . . .'

If this was not the language the Labour Front Bench would have used, they must certainly have applauded the sentiment. The sudden confluence of Conservative paternalism with socialist ethics produced a wave of assent that very nearly got the amendment passed, and the fact that it was defeated by only eight votes led to some recrimination against the bishops for hanging their gloves up before the fight was over. Lord Stockton's criticisms of the Bill did not go to waste, however, for reasons that became clear a few days later.

The spring of 1986 was not a comfortable time for the Government. On the fourth and final day of the Bill's Committee Stage in the Lords, 23rd January came another reminder of the unpopularity in Ulster of the Anglo-Irish Agreement. In the by-elections, which were widely hailed as a referendum on the Government's Northern Ireland policy, fourteen of the fifteen MPs were resoundingly returned to their seats, the fifteenth – Jim Nicholson of the DUP – being ousted by the SDLP.

Back at Westminster, the Prime Minister was making a statement about the Westland Affair. Subsequent to Michael Heseltine's resignation the Government had instituted an inquiry into the circumstances surrounding the leaking of Sir

Patrick Mayhew's letter. The Defence Secretary's statement had accused Leon Brittan of betraying the Government's officialy impartial stance on the Westland takeover by telling Sir Raymond Lygo, managing director of British Aerospace, that his company's involvement in the European consortium would be 'against the national interest'. He had also hinted darkly at a cover-up by Margaret Thatcher. The inquiry placed responsibility for the leak squarely on the shoulders of Leon Brittan; however, it was known that the leak came from No. 10 Downing Street and not Leon Brittan's own department, and this naturally provoked speculation as to the Prime Minister's role in the affair.

In her statement to the Commons Margaret Thatcher said that in retrospect she agreed with Leon Brittan that it had been 'a matter of duty' that the Mayhew letter be leaked before 4pm on 6th January.

However she had not been consulted by Leon Brittan over the use of her own office as a source for the leak, nor by her staff, although they had 'correctly considered' that she would agree. The upshot of the affair was that the Prime Minister received a barracking in the Commons, Leon Brittan resigned, and the confidence of the Conservative Party – not boosted by its poor showing in the Tyne Bridge by-election just before Christmas – was substantially shaken.

The Campaign, meanwhile, was having problems of a different kind.

It had been noted at the Steering Committee meeting on 17th January that we were using up Michael Windridge's time at a rate of more than five executive days per week. If we wanted to retain his services for the duration of the four month contract this meant one of two things; either he cut his commitment back to two days or we had to find more cash. Everyone agreed that Extel had proved a sound investment, and that if we could possibly afford to we should extend the consultancy. In the end the decision was taken to keep Extel until 14th February, and to review the situation monthly from then on. But that didn't solve the financial crisis. We had only afforded Extel's services anyway by borrowing the very limited funds of the Jubilee Centre, and by the next meeting on 31st January it was clear that it we were going to carry on we would have to appeal to some of the retailers on whose behalf the Campaign was being conducted. Accordingly it was agreed that the question of finance should be raised at a retailers' luncheon Viscount Brentford was putting on in the House of Lords the following week.

The Bill survived its Committee Stage in the Lords without amendment, and the Report Stage was duly scheduled for 6th and 11th February. That gave Lord Graham and the Jubilee Centre an interlude in which to adjust and improve the amendments – taking account of the objections raised to them in the previous debate – so that they could be put forward again before the Bill had its Third Reading and was handed over to the Commons.

In the meantime, on 28th January, the celebrated Clive Ponting trial had opened. Ponting had been charged under Section 2 of the 1911 Official Secrets Act for passing on information – including one document classified as confidential – to Tam Dalyell MP, although Tam Dalyell 'was not a person to whom he was authorised to communicate it or to whom it was his duty to do so in the interests of the state'. The information concerned had to do with the sinking of the Argentinian cruiser *General Belgrano* during the Falklands Conflict of 1982. The then Defence Secretary, John Nott, had told the House of Commons afterwards that the cruiser had been 'closing' on the British Task Force at the time, and was thus a legitimate target. Ponting's information cast doubt on this, and thus on the motives of the Government in allowing the attack to take place. Giving evidence on 5th February, Clive Ponting claimed that it was 'in the wider interests of Parliament to be told how it was being misled and how the Government was proposing to mislead it'.

The judge, Mr Justice McCowan, told the jury that while this was a matter for mitigation in sentencing, it was not relevant to the determination of guilt. The jury disagreed; and on 11th February Clive Ponting was acquitted – this resulting in considerable embarrassment for the Government, and some sharp exchanges in the Commons between Margaret Thatcher and Neil Kinnock over the definition of national security.

It was on the afternoon of the same day, at the Report Stage of the Shops Bill, that Lord Denning moved Amendment No. 10.

Clause 2 of the Shops Bill ran as follows:

Sections 17, 19, 21, 22 and 23 of the Shops Act 1950 (half-holidays, meal times and Sunday employment of shop assistants and others employed in connection with retail trades and businesses) shall cease to apply for the purpose of regulating the employment of persons who have attained the age of eighteen.

What Lord Denning proposed was the simple replacement of the word 'cease' by the word 'continue', thus in effect retaining a substantial part of the 1950 Act and scrapping the whole second clause of the Bill. It had been inspired by Baroness Camden's amendment at Committee Stage, and in particular by the Earl of Stockton's statement in the course of the ensuing debate that even 'if this amendment is not the right method' some way should be found of protecting shopworkers' rights. As possibly the most revered establishment figures in the Lords neither man had seemed a likely ally in the Sunday trading dispute. But if the Earl of Stockton had rocked the boat, Lord Denning seemed set on rolling it clean over.

Having, he explained, examined the 'sensible provisions' of the 1950 Act, he had studied the Auld Report to find out what inspired the Government to get rid of them.

'In paragraph 295 they quite rightly start by saying: "In our view it would be unfortunate if the Government were to remove all the protection that shopworkers have . . . at the very moment when, if our recommendations were to be adopted, they would feel at their most vulnerable."

'This is all very sensible. Then they go on to say: "At the same time, we believe it would be wrong to continue in statutory form the special and inflexible provision for adult shopworkers, some of them only applicable to shopworkers in England and Wales."

'Then they say: "It may be that the answer lies in the extension of the role now exercised by the Wages Councils to ensure not only adequate pay but also satisfactory conditions of employment.'' '

The problem was that legislation before the Commons on the same afternoon proposed a muzzling of the Wages Councils' power. Lord Campbell replied to the speech by drawing attention to the Government Amendment (No 19) which, because it dealt with the same issue, was being considered simultaneously with Lord Denning's. This provided for a two year moratorium during which the Government would undertake to retain the parts of the Shops Act referred to in Clause 2 of the Bill. As Lord Rochester pointed out, however, the moratorium carried no assurance of review; its only effect would be to push implementation of the measure safely beyond the next election.

Lord Oram summed up the situation.

'Below the eighteenth birthday of the shopworker, he will continue to have the protection afforded at present by the 1950 Act. After his twenty-first birthday he will receive the protection of a wages council. However that wages council will be a very much weaker body than the present Wages Council. In between the eighteenth and twenty-first birthday, a retail worker will have no statutory protection at all.'

Here was an anomaly in the Government's own proposals. Various speakers then proceeded to denounce the Government's policy as 'total nonsense' and 'absolutely unenforceable'. Lord McCarthy even went so far as to suggest that Amendment No 19 was being considered here – and not at Committee Stage – because the Government wanted to deflect the force of Lord Denning's amendment. Lord Glenarthur, whose job it was to steer the Bill through the Lords, attempted to rationalize the Government's position.

Hansard, the official record of proceedings in the Houses of Parliament, gives the ensuing exchange as follows:

> *Lord Glenarthur:* 'With regard to the wages council legislation . . . the Wages Board deals primarily with pay, and evidence suggests that the current wage rates – the noble Lord, Lord McCarthy, shakes his head, but nevertheless there is evidence – inhibit the employment of young people up to the age of twenty-one.

79

Lord Graham: There is no evidence, my Lords.

Lord Glenarthur: My Lords, the noble Lord, Lord Graham, says that there is no evidence. There is evidence to support it.

Noble Lords: Produce it!

At 4.27 pm Lord Denning moved his amendment, and it was carried by just one vote.

The Government's amendment, No 19, was not moved.

Chapter 7

Roses for Westminster

The Bill amended/Operation Valentine/The backlash/Arguments for Sunday opening: criminal law, retail response, Scotland

The Denning amendment was a major defeat for the Government. The fact that it had been achieved at Report Stage also made it hard to overturn, and although there were rumours initially that the Government might attempt to reverse it at Third Reading, within the next forty-eight hours word filtered through to Conservative backbenchers that the amendment would be allowed to stand.

The main result of it was the destruction of Clause 2 – the part of the Bill designed to remove legal restrictions against employment of labour (as opposed to the opening of shops) on Sunday, and which would also – quite unnecessarily – have deprived shopworkers of their statutory right to meal breaks and half-holidays. With Clause 2 gone the Bill became self-contradictory; because although under Lord Denning's amendment the protection afforded by the 1950 Act continued to apply to shopworkers of every age, Schedule 2 clearly stated that this protection applied only to sixteen and seventeen year olds.

The fact that the amendment was passed at all was owing in large measure to the impact the Earl of Stockton's speech had made on the Conservative Party. His point that the Bill's purpose was to 'make it possible for people to trade on Sundays' and not to 'make life more difficult for shop assistants' had roused the conscience of some peers for whom the true ideal of Conservatism was not an unfettered free market, but a capitalism of compassion. The point was rubbed in soon afterwards by Cardinal Hume in a letter to *The Times:*

81

It is a Government's duty to mediate between particular conflicting interests for the sake of the common good. To abandon the task on the pretext that it is too difficult is to surrender the function of government.

We must beware lest the principle prevail that the market should rule supreme seven days a week. Our principle is that there is more to being human than supply and demand; there is more to social life than trading and commerce.

This pressure, coming as it did not just from the church but from the Government's own political tradition, produced a second concession in the Lords.

After the Earl of Stockton's speech at Committee Stage an amendment had been proposed by Lord Renton which tried to ameliorate a rather too sharp distinction in the Bill's first Schedule between existing and future shopworkers. As Lord Wolfson said, under these conditions an existing shopworker who changed jobs in the retail industry would lose a statutory protection which he was surely entitled to retain. This criticism, and the general view that Schedule 1 was anyway, to quote Lord Renton, 'a bit of a jumble', resulted in the Government striking a deal; if Lord Renton withdrew the amendment – which might well have been passed – Schedule 1 would be redrafted to extend the rights of the existing shopworker who wanted to move from one retailing job to another. This was done, and the revised first Schedule was accepted (uncontroversially now, because it was a Government amendment) on the same afternoon as Lord Denning's.

Of course the Bill's main provision – to deregulate shopping hours – remained intact, and neither amendment weakened the Government's resolve to push this through. When news of the day's proceedings in the Upper House arrived in the Commons Gerald Kaufman demanded to know if the Bill was now going to be dropped. It wasn't; in the words of the Paymaster General, Kenneth Clarke, the suggestion was 'quite absurd'.

Outside Parliament the most noticeable result was a highlighting of the Government's vulnerability, something that led to a good deal of discussion in the papers. Opinion was divided; for some commentators the demise of Clause 2 sounded a warning bell; to quote the *Guardian* leader (13th February) however laudable the reasons for introducing the legislation had been when Leon Brittan's writ ran at the Home Office, 'the objections, the slightly sneaky bits and the political worries' were starting to 'bear in on Mr Brittan's successors'. Others adopted the less demanding pose of moral outrage. Thus, according to the *Daily Mail* (13th February):

> The Shops Bill, the whole Bill, and nothing but the Bill – that should be the Government's rallying cry. On this most populist of issues, the grocer's daughter, from Grantham cannot let the peers thwart the will of the people.

It was against this background, three days after the Denning amendment, that Operation Valentine began. Strenuous efforts on the part of Tim Law and his team of co-ordinators had enabled the Campaign to stage over two hundred constituency meetings; respectably close, anyway, to the number that had made such an impression on me a year before when I read the story of Gideon. In fact not all of the 'We love Sunday' meetings happened on 14th February. In some constituencies, if the MP was unable to attend on that date, the meeting was scheduled for the week before or the week after. Nevertheless before the end of February 30,000 people across the country had turned out to make their views on Sunday trading known, and in well over half the constituencies the MP – who was often, but not always, a Conservative – had been there to hear them.

The meeting in Guildford was fairly representative of the kind of events staged by the local organisers. Alec Frame, whom I had met for the first time at our weekend conference the previous September, had put a lot of emphasis on publicity. Handbills were printed and distributed, announcements made in the press and on the radio, invitations issued not just among the churches but also to employees of the larger shops. In the end, and rather to Alec Frame's surprise, over 400 people crammed into Bishop Reindoorp Church of England School to question the Conservative MP

David Howell. Care had been taken to select a neutral and widely respected chairman – the recently retired chief executive of Guildford Borough Council – and if David Howell maintained adamantly that he had as many people pressing him to support the Shops Bill as to vote against it, he nonetheless went on to abstain at the Bill's Second Reading.

Aubrey Roberts, co-ordinator for fifteen constituencies in the south, had two speakers on the platform in St Alban's: Parliamentary Private Secretary Peter Lilley MP and Bishop John Taylor. Since a recent meeting on the abortion issue had attracted only sixty, an attendance of 508 over Sunday trading was a credit to the energy and ingenuity of the meeting's organisers. Once again much sound preparation had gone into the event; money had been raised locally, and a glossy colour insert sent out in a local free newspaper. Because Peter Lilley was only able to stay for an hour (he arrived in a dinner suit, having left his wife at a Valentine's dance), most of the questions – which came from supporters as well as opponents of the Bill – were fielded by the Bishop. But the discussion did not go to waste; Aubrey Roberts had the last part of the meeting recorded and sent to Peter Lilley at Westminster. He also managed to extend his press coverage by conducting a poll and publishing the results in the local paper.

Guildford and St Alban's were indicative of the Campaign's reliance on local initiative to make Operation Valentine work. The Jubilee Centre provided back-up and gave guidelines on protocol; for instance, while the attempt was made in every case to represent on the platform a diversity of community interests, the MP was always consulted beforehand about the choice of local speakers and given the option of appearing alone if preferred. Concerning the meetings in general a number of features stood out. For one thing, in comparison to most constituency meetings – which often attracted less than fifty participants – they were extremely well attended: the numbers regularly exceeded 100 and sometimes, as in Bath, approached 1,000. Also, although we took care to advertise the meetings widely, those who came were nearly all against the Bill, and although the trade unions and retail organisations were well represented, by far the majority came from the churches.

Naturally, there was a danger here of associating the Campaign too strongly with the popular and inaccurate notion of 'Sabbatarianism', and this wasn't helped by questions that dwelt on the biblical case against Sunday trading; for all the wealth of applicable texts an MP who supported the Bill usually did so on social and economic grounds and simply failed to see their relevance. But a total breakdown of communication was rare; in most cases the impression made was of lively and well-informed constituency concern; and if some staunch supporters of deregulation, like Cyril Townsend MP, left confirmed in their feeling that the Bill was opposed mainly by 'puritanical' Christians, a good many of those in the middle ground were inclined to think their position over.

David Crouch, MP for Canterbury, was sufficiently moved by his experience to write to *The Times* about it. Like 400 other Conservatives – as well as all Social Democrats, Liberal and members of the Labour Shadow Cabinet – he had received on Valentines Day morning a single red rose and a giant Valentine card. This he could easily have dismissed as a publicity stunt pulled off by a group of enthusiastic but extreme churchmen. However, at the constituency meeting that night he found that:

. . . in addition to many churchgoers, the audience contained many retail employers and shop assistants.

I argued the case for Sunday trading. I pointed out the present anomalies whereby it is a criminal offence to sell so many things that we have come to regard as reasonable, and certainly not improper. . . The law was an ass and we should tidy it up and allow Sunday trading.

The other speakers were a canon, a trade unionist and an employer. They were all strongly opposed to the idea. When it came to questions from the audience of over 200 no one supported me. To make sure I was in no doubt about their views the chairman called for a vote on a show of hands. Not a single hand was raised in my support.

The message is clear and I agree with my colleague William van Straubenzee, we do have to listen to the electorate. We should tidy up the anomalies but not go for complete deregulation. I believe my electors would accept legislation of additional Sunday shopping at garden centres, DIY centres and motor factors (for vehicle spare parts) – and we should leave it at that.

How an MP responded to the Campaign lobby depended on a variety of things, including the size of his electoral majority and the nature of his political convictions. No MP changed his mind lightly; but in view of the pressures bearing on his decision, and of the success of Operation Valentine in emphasising the strength of public feeling against the Bill, it was understandable that the Campaign's opponents came to put it down as a 'vociferous and well-organised minority'. In fact this was a description apt for the core group of any movement – social, political or religious – including Britain's two main political parties. The question really was not how few people were motivated enough to become activists, but whether their ideas were laudable and expressive of the desires and wishes of the population. Consequently, the point was well taken that Viscount Tonypandy made in a letter published alongside that of David Crouch: 'If the Government are so confident that there is a public clamour for change in Sunday legislation, why do they not withdraw the present Shops Bill and put this proposal into their next election manifesto?'

That they were not confident was evidenced by the battle that ensured in the media. The Government's counter-offensive came right from the top. 'Ministers,' said the *Guardian* (22nd February) 'are being urged by Downing Street and Mr Norman Tebbit, the Conservative Party Chairman, to confront the fears of those who oppose the trading measure.' Accordingly, Douglas Hurd wrote to Conservative MPs almost immediately after Operation Valentine, explaining the Government's position and urging them to support the Bill. The media assault followed on 21st February. In a speech in Scunthorpe the Home Secretary told his audience that the Shops Bill was a 'sensible and pragmatic attempt to reform the law'; he went on, 'Sundays will, I believe, continue to be a day different from other days because the majority of the British people want it to be, not because the law tells them that it is.' On the same evening, addressing a meeting in Bath, Lord Young tackled the effects of the new legislation on shopworkers: 'We must not allow emotional arguments to cloud this issue,' he said. 'We are not making either the opening of shops nor the working in them compulsory.'

Elsewhere sweet reasonableness was sometimes laid aside in favour of the vitriol. Appearing in a live debate on ITV's *Daytime* Home Office Minister David Waddington condemned the whole case against deregulation as 'bogus'. He had no time for economic models predicting the effect of seven day trading on the market place ('Let us face facts,' he said. 'Shops open and shops close according to when individual small traders decide they will work.'); nor for the views of the USDAW representative who felt the Shops Bill was designed to erode the law for shopkeepers ('the most bogus point I have heard in my life'). Finally he turned his attention to me. I had floated a compromise measure allowing some Sunday opening for DIY and garden stores, and shops with under four workers on their payroll. 'Arrant rubbish,' declared David Waddington roundly; and since numerous small retailers would clearly sack staff in order to slip in under the wire, also 'a marvellous recipe for unemployment'.

To be fair to David Waddington there was more to the programme than the choice phrases he selected to disparage the views of the Campaign; but such was the flavour of the debate, and in that respect it signified a shift in the pace of the whole Sunday dispute.

The debate was warming up.

In the following days a number of arguments for the Shops Bill came to the fore.

To anyone who had bothered to think over the issue it was apparent by now that the questions raised by Sunday trading were many and complex. Complexity, however, had never been a virtue in the fast-moving world of the publicity man; here the battle between truth and falsehood was settled not on the basis of merit, but of 'image'. Consequently the arguments put forward by Government spokesmen and other proponents of the Bill were apt to sacrifice intellectual integrity for the sake of impact on public opinion.

For example in his letter to Conservative MPs after Operation Valentine the Home Secretary wrote:

> The real point is not whether Christians and most sensible people want to keep Sunday special. It is whether the criminal law is the right method for bringing this about.

Of course 'most sensible people' would have objected strongly at the thought of a poor, struggling shopkeeper miserably defending his sale of a tin of dried milk on a Sunday under the ominous gaze of a judge for whom leniency meant five years' hard labour. But the term 'criminal law' was here being misused in exactly the same way as the term 'Sabbatarian'; of course there was a valid discussion to be had about the appropriateness of using one or another branch of the law to regulate Sunday trading, but for some people who wanted the restrictions removed completely that was beside the point – for them the chief value of the term was its insinuation of a heavy-handed penalty for a trivial offence.

In fact the criminal law fell into two distinct branches. In one, which covered most of what is popularly conceived of as 'criminal' activity – murder, rape, theft and so on – it has to be proved not only that the defendant committed the crime, but that the crime included a *mens rea*, or a mental element – which often, though not always, had to do with motive. In the other branch of criminal law this *mens rea* was assumed to exist, and to determine guilt the court required proof only that the defendant did what he was accused of. Since this covered a wide range of less serious offences – the sale of bad meat, breaking the speed limit, cycling at night without working front and rear lights – to find Sunday opening classified as a criminal offence was not very remarkable. The only other option was to make it a civil offence, and since the civil law (very broadly speaking) covered wrongs against individuals rather than wrongs against society as a whole, there was little to be gained by change – after all, it could seldom be said that a shop opening on a Sunday was wronging a particular individual.

Another argument in support of deregulation claimed that the passing of a new Shops Act would make only a slight difference to existing patterns of Sunday opening. According to the IFS study, shops accounting for no more than forty-eight percent of total turnover would take advantage of their new freedom. In his speech recommending the Auld Report to Parliament Leon Brittan quoted a figure of twenty to thirty percent. He didn't say how he arrived at this, but it was supported by the results of a survey (carried out by Terry Burke of the Business Studies Faculty at the Polytechnic of Central London in early 1985) which predicted that fifteen to twenty percent of high street shopping centres would adopt Sunday opening, along with most out-of-town centres.

Such estimates were reassuring. However they rested on a rather rosy view of the retail sector. Terry Burke himself said that high street multiples would open 'if they consider it likely to be profitable or as a reaction to competitive pressures and fears of loss of market share'. This was a crucial admission. It meant that the economic pressures on a retailer could only ever work towards the extension of opening hours, and consequently that his staying closed on a Sunday depended on such pressures being negligible or wholly absent. In practice, to make such an assumption was hopelessly unrealistic; retailing had become an intensely competitive business; and not only that, but if the Wages Bill became law there would no longer be a legal requirement to pay staff double time on Sundays, and trading on Sunday would be more financially attractive. Hardly surprising, then, that according to the John Lewis Partnership 'Sunday opening would become progressive and irresistible'. It would happen eventually just as surely as a ball on a slope would roll downhill.

At this point the supporters of seven day trading produced their trump card: Scotland. No matter how uncertain the theoretical grounds for stability in Sunday opening, the fact was that in Scotland, where it was already legal, a 1985 MORI survey had showed eighty-four percent of shops to be shut on a Sunday and ninety-eight percent of shoppers to be 'not personally inconvenienced' by Sunday trading.

What better test case could there be for deregulation in England and Wales?

This was shallow thinking, to say the least. For one thing, as we already knew, the low incidence of Sunday opening in Scotland depended directly on the fact that national high street multiples were forced to close in the rest of the country. A typical high street multiple had between five and ten percent of its stores north of the border; so even if competition in Scotland deprived those stores of say, ten percent of their trade (a very high estimate), the loss to the whole retail chain would work out at only 0.5 to one percent of its total trade. So the decision to stay closed in Scotland, and the decison to stay closed in England and Wales, were different in terms of pure accountancy. Pretending that a multiple would transfer its Scottish policy directly to Sunday opening in the country as a whole was about as illogical as planting tropical shrubs out in the garden because they flourished in the greenhouse; eighty-four percent of Scottish shops stayed closed on Sunday because of the special economic conditions prevailing in Scotland – conditions which could never prevail across the country as a whole, and which could cease to prevail in Scotland the moment the Shops Bill became law.

Of course there were other factors contributing to the peculiar nature of the Scottish retail climate, not least the characteristics of the country itself. That there was a greater built-in resistance to Sunday trading on cultural and religious grounds was the factor on the strength of which earlier legislators thought it unnecessary to include Scotland under the 1950 Act. Which went to show how tempting, and yet naive, it was to draw parallels between different cultures and then use them as proof that what worked in one must necessarily work in another – after all, the Jubilee Centre's Good Friday survey had already indicated that Sunday opening would increase more dramatically in the rest of Britain than it had done in Scotland. Significantly, the Auld Committee, which had examined the Scottish situation, stated that as far as predicting the effects of deregulation in England and Wales was concerned:

Our overriding conclusion from our review of the

experience of other countries is that their economic, social and historial traditions vary so much that none could provide a reliable guide. . .

The Government had confidence enough in the Report's other conclusions. They were curiously silent about this one.

Chapter 8

No Alternative

Finding friends in the Commons/The Second EDM/The problem of alternatives to total deregulation/Campaign policy on alternatives/The Second Reading delayed/Parliamentary lobbies/The USDAW petition and the Harris Poll/A word from Lord Gnome/Finance – again/The end of the term.

As February neared its end, Ivor Stanbrook was running into trouble.

To defeat the Shops Bill at Second Reading, or just to get a reasonable representation on the Standing Committee, would require support from all quarters of the House. Both the Liberal Party and the SDP had indicated they would have a free vote; the Labour Party has not made a final decision. But Ivor Stanbrook's difficulty did not lie so much in persuading other MPs to vote against the Bill as in getting them into the House to do it. A full turnout was likely only if the opposition parties smelled a Government defeat, and MPs' estimate of the chances of this kind of upset occurring rested heavily on Conservative response to the Early Day Motion Ann Winterton had put down before Christmas; 100 signatures on that would be virtually decisive. As of 14th February, however, there were only fifty-five, and not all of these were Conservatives. Clearly another mechanism was needed to muster opposition. Accordingly, and in the hope of defining a general position against the Bill at which MPs of all parties could meet, Ivor Stanbrook began the delicate business of negotiating with Labour's shadow Home Secretary Gerald Kaufman on the wording of an all-party reasoned amendment.

Within the Conservative Party itself opposition was strong, but not quite strong enough. Ivor Stanbrook was regularly having fifty Conservative backbenchers at his meetings, and knew that another twenty were sympathetic; if in addition to a full turnout from the other parties all of these voted against the Bill, the Ayes and Noes would be almost exactly balanced. In reality, however, he had to contend both with the probability that many would abstain rather than vote against, and with the power of the Whips. By signing Ann Winterton's EDM numerous Conservatives had affirmed their view of Sunday trading as a matter for individual conscience – but that did not guarantee they would defy a Government three-liner. It was necessary therefore to provide a vehicle to register dissent specifically on the Sunday issue, and to this end, on 24th February, Ivor Stanbrook put down a second EDM.

This called on the Government to amend the Bill 'to preserve the special character of Sunday and to have regard for the principles and conscience of those who would be affected by the total deregulation of Sunday trading'. Since anyone who signed this could almost certainly be relied upon to vote against the Bill, comparing the signatories on each EDM provided a useful guide to opinion on the Back Bench. There were, after all, many MPs whose nominal support for the rebels over the conscience issue might – if they knew what else was at stake – be pushed into outright opposition. What Ivor Stanbrook needed was the opportunity to talk to them. Time being at a premium the assistance of some of the 'younger' Parliamentarians like Tony Marlowe and Peter Brunivels proved extremely valuable, and the rapid increase in signatures on the second EDM was largely owing to their efforts.

Here, however, Ivor Stanbrook faced a crucial difficulty. On the EDM's central proposition – that the Shops Bill in its present form was unacceptable – it was relatively easy to build up a wide base of support. Labour MPs in general, and MPs sponsored by USDAW and the Co-op in particular, objected to the Bill because of its effect on workers; this was important to many Conservative MPs as well, and even a lot of backbenchers not used to championing the cause of the underprivileged were willing to oppose the Bill on religious grounds or through pique at the Government's use of the whip. But to say, as everyone did, that the law needed changing, and at the same time to say that the Shops Bill did not make the right changes, raised at once the far more divisive question of what should be put in its place. In the hope that presenting an alternative would strengthen their support, the rebels met on several occasions to hammer out an acceptable compromise. They failed. And this exerted pressure on the Campaign.

The problem was discussed vigorously at three consecutive meetings of the Steering Committee in February. There were really two questions: one, whether a viable alternative to total deregulation could be found; and two, whether an alternative could be found that everyone agreed on.

The Auld Committee had examined and rejected a number of so-called 'half-way houses'. 'The analysis', said Leon Brittan, 'is either indefensible or unworkable.' Devasting was perhaps not as apt a word as dubious. The relevant chapter of the Report concluded confidently:

> . . .we are convinced that none of the suggestions for reform, short of complete abolition of restrictions, would work. None of them would work because they would not form the basis of a fair, simple and readily enforceable system of regulation.

This platonic ideal of a law that was 'fair, simple and readily enforceable' inevitably made all practicable proposals look rather shoddy. What the Auld Committee failed to point out was that against the standard of perfection their own proposal looked as bad as the rest. Probably worse, for with respect to the matter of fairness they insisted: 'In our view, all forms of control canvassed in our Inquiry, while affording protection to some, would neglect the interests of others'. Of course it was perfectly true to say that no alternative solution protected everyone equally, but it was nonsense (as well as a dereliction of moral duty) to make this an excuse for protecting no one. What that really amounted to was neglect of the poor and weak in favour of the wealthy and strong – hardly 'fair' by any reckoning.

As for simplicity and enforceability, it stood to reason that no law had ever been absolutely simple or absolutely enforceable. What mattered was to make the alternative solution simple and enforceable *enough* to work in practice. That this could be achieved was evident from the fact that every European country except Sweden already had satisfactory laws regulating Sunday trading. In France, for example, before a shop could open on a Sunday, standard procedure required an agreement between the employer, the employees, and the district Prefect. Norway allowed Sunday trading in the afternoon, Luxembourg until 1pm and on condition that the shop close on Monday morning to compensate. The Netherlands, Belgium, Finland, Greece, Switzerland, Austria, Denmark and West Germany all had general prohibitions on Sunday trading which in the last three cases extended to cover Saturday afternoons as well.

A number of alternatives for the British situation were on the table. Two fairly straightforward ones used time: either by prohibiting trade before 1pm, or allowing shops at the managers' discretion but not for more than four hours. Another proposed a limitation on the size of a shop, generally defined in terms of number of employees (the Jubilee Centre had developed a hybrid version of this, favouring small shops but giving special consideration to DIY and garden centres), and still another by a redrafting of the list of exempted goods. It was also feasible to follow the Italian example and leave the regulation of Sunday trading not to Parliament but to the local authorities.

From a long and wearisome discussion of the pros and cons of these various ideas two facts emerged. One was that while any alternative was fairer than total deregulation, no alternative was equally fair to all. In other words, as we had discovered before when we published *How To Tidy Up The Law*, it was well nigh impossible to find one option that everyone could back. By the end of the afternoon on 21st February the Drapers' Chamber of Trade was leaning towards the 1pm option, the British Hardware Federation towards the Four Hour Option, and the NCT towards its own original draft Bill. It was the classic weakness of coalition.

The second fact was perhaps the more telling. In public debate nothing was harder than defending your own concrete proposal, and nothing easier than destroying someone else's – David Waddington's treatment of the Small Shops Option on ITV had illustrated that only too clearly. The upshot was that falling in behind one option and making it the Campaign's official policy would, strategically, be a very unwise move. True we'd have an answer to the taunt that nobody agreed on an alternative; but there was more to be lost than gained in terms of the publicity battle we would only be putting another weapon in the Government's hand. Accordingly, Lord Brentford suggested that the Campaign should not give its official endorsement to any single amendment of the Bill. There were mixed feelings on the Committee. USDAW's representative, John Flood, was strongly in favour of flexibility; Leslie Seeney agreed strongly with Lord Brentford that total opposition to the Bill was the only way forward. The meeting was adjourned until 28th February.

Since Operation Valentine the Campaign had made rapid progress. Our launch in Wales on 21st February had been well covered in the local newspapers, and we were now getting plenty of attention in Scotland, where the Pro-Sunday Coalition's distribution of the leaflet *Your Sunday Is About To Be Hijacked* had been followed by discussions on television and radio, and correspondence in the *Glasgow Herald*. Nationwide, alongside the Keep Sunday Special Campaign, representations had been made by retailers like the John Lewis Partnership and both national and local trade associaitons had been lobbying MPs – a grassroots pressure emphasised by the fact that Parliamentary questions on 20th February had again highlighted the success of the letter-writing campaign: 37,317 against the Bill to 317 in favour. The point wasn't lost on the media; in fact by the end of the month the publicity given to the deregulation dispute was causing DIY stores like B&Q in Bristol to stay closed on Sundays for fear of prosecution, and eliciting words of caution from the national press. Thus the *Daily Telegraph* leader on 3rd March:

> Generally speaking, measures which outrage the deep feelings of large sections of the community and command the enthusiastic support of doctrinaires and a few large commercial institutions do not make good politics. . .

96

democracy is ill-served by politicians who are insensitive to public feeling.

On 25th February the Shops Bill completed its Third Reading in the Lords. Because Lord Graham had been so successful in delaying the Bill's progress through the Upper House there was every chance that Ministers would try to push it into the Commons before the Easter Recess at the end of March. If they did, and if the Government used the three-line whip, we calculated that under present conditions we'd still be in for a fairly heavy defeat. Whatever time remained therefore now had to be used to maximum advantage.

I reviewed our recent initiatives with Michael Windridge. A few days earlier we had acted on an idea that had also occurred to John Flood of USDAW. The situation in Northern Ireland had changed little since the by-elections. Despite an apparently conciliatory meeting between Mrs Thatcher and Ulster's political leaders plans for a province-wide one day stoppage were going ahead, and the fourteen Ulster Unionist MPs had still not taken up their seats at Westminster. They were, however, keen to register in whatever way they could the unacceptability of the Anglo-Irish Agreement to the Protestant majority in Ulster, and there was a slim chance that some of them, at least, might agree to return to Parliament for the Second Reading of the Shops Bill if there was a chance of embarassing the Prime Minister. Sir Bernard Braine had accordingly undertaken to write to them.

Of more immediate importance, plans had now been finalised for four Parliamentary lobbies at the beginning of March. These replaced the mass rally at Westminster Central Hall we had envisaged as following up Operation Valentine; they were, in brief, a lot less trouble and a better investment in terms of publicity and influence on the people whose opinion really mattered – the MPs. To stage them the Grand Committee Room at Westminister had been booked for 6th and 7th March and arrangements made for handfuls of constituents to meet ninety selected Members of Parliament and make known in a setting more informal than the constituency meetings or surgeries their misgivings about the

Shops Bill. In the course of the meeting each MP would be given the petition raised in his or her constituency and asked to lay it before the House of Commons, ensuring that the action was recorded in the daily Order Paper. They would all be asked to sign Ivor Stanbrook's EDM, oppose the Second Reading of the Bill, and ask the Home Office why the Auld Committee had not examined the shopping regulations in Europe.

In the event of an early Second Reading these two initiatives might have more direct effect than the national petition, which at an estimated total of over 700,000 signatures was getting so big that the Jubilee Centre was going to have to borrow an entire church hall to collate it. Our hope was to have it presented to the Home Secretary by a delegation of leading churchmen, but so far we had no firm indication either from the Home Office or the churches that this would be possible. We didn't even know if it would be ready in time.

Consequently what happened a week later was greeted with a mixture of consternation and relief. The Committee met as arranged on 28th February, and finally affirmed Lord Brentford's policy of not putting forward a specific amendment before Second Reading; the stoppage in Northern Ireland went ahead on 3rd March with 655 road blocks, 237 reports of intimidation, and fifty-seven arrests; on 5th March the first constituency petition against the Shops Bill was presented in the Commons by David Amess, MP. And then, unexpectedly, on the day of the first Parliamentrary lobby, news broke that the Bill's Second Reading had been delayed.

Why, after rushing the legislation through, the Government suddenly decided to use the delaying tactic themselves wasn't clear. Ivor Stanbrook took it as a good omen. As he told reporters the next morning: 'I am much more optimistic now. Both as a result of the decision to delay the Bill, and in conversations with Ministers, I believe they are sincerely trying to accommodate us if possible.' More cynical campaigners inclined to the view that the Government, sensing the swell of opinion against the Bill after Operation Valentine, were using consultation over alternative proposals as an excuse for marking time until the waters receded.

When the Steering Committee met again on 7th March it

was to hear Michael Windridge declare the Parliamentary lobbies a modest but definite success. Two hundred constituency members had attended, photographs had been taken – particularly of Neil Kinnock hugging a couple of young Keep Sunday Special supporters – and one MP, Barry Porter, who had backed the Auld Report, told his constituents that he would be voting against the Bill. Perhaps more significant, in less than two weeks the second EDM had been signed by ninety-two MPs, and in a meeting with rebel back-benchers the Prime Minister herself had indicated her willingness to consider alternatives to total deregulation – indeed she had said that the Home Office was considering them already.

In light of these developments we were obliged to re-examine our strategy.

The Open Shop Group, who at first seemed to have been caught napping in the correspondence race, were now canvassing support among their customers, and unlike the Keep Sunday Special Campaign – which had merely encouraged people to write to their MPs and told them how to do it – were using form letters in an attempt to close the gap. We had discussed the method ourselves at the Jubilee Centre, and the members of the Steering Committee agreed with our conclusion that it looked phoney, and was consequently self-defeating. Nevertheless we felt we would probably need to boost our own letter campaign, and so the decision was taken to produce as cheaply as possible tens of thousands of leaflets encouraging another write-in to MPs before the Second Reading.

Since we now anticipated a protracted fight in the Commons, it was thought advisable to plan on a longer-term basis. We confirmed arrangements for a meeting on 15th March with our constituency activists – most of whom even Tim Law only knew as voices on the end of a phone line – designed to promote personal contact, give the campaign more cohesion, and to get further ideas for constituency level publicity. Further ahead, probably the beginning of May, we laid sketchy plans for a series of local rallies. There was an acute sense now of the need to pace ourselves; the Campaign had been going for three months and the Jubilee Centre had been at full stretch for the best part of a year. We knew that by the time another two months had gone by, no matter how much attention we got in the press, fatigue would start to set in.

Happily, events over the next fortnight or so shifted the balance of the debate slightly in our favour.

7th March had also seen the tragic death of the Conservative MP for Fulham, Martin Stevens. In the year before a General Election another by-election challenge was not a welcome prospect for the Government; the Conservatives had slumped from first to third in Brecon and Radnor in July of the previous year, and from second to third at Tyne Bridge in December. Losing in Fulham would pose no threat to the Government's overall majority, and affect only marginally the arithmetic of the Second Reading on the Shops Bill; but it would shake the backbench confidence in the Party leadership, and make more likely a gesture of independence of the sort that had occured recently over the privatisation of British Leyland, when ten backbenchers, including Edward Heath had abstained.

Also, the Campaign's lobbying of MPs had produced a flurry of correspondence in the national papers, expressing a range of opinion both on the Sunday dispute and how it might be resolved. Though the corrspondence dropped off again the following week the strength of opposition to the Shops Bill was marked in two ways. First, on Monday 10th March, John Flood presented the 300,000 strong USDAW petition to Buckingham Palace, calling on the Queen to support the shopworker's rights against what the union regarded as an 'unconstitutional' Bill. And second – perhaps just as important, though less widely reported – the Campaign published the results of the Harris Poll commissioned through the Pro-Sunday Coalition.

We had prepared this survey carefully to avoid as many as possible of the biases inherent in rapid assessments of public opinion. But of course it was designed to prove a point, and the questions we asked yielded answers strikingly different from those obtained by Open Shop, or the National Consumer Council whose Chairman Rachel Waterhouse had claimed in a letter to *The Times* on 24th February that: 'Poll after poll of statistically representative samples of the public shows the majority of people to be in favour of deregulation'. In our survey, out of a total of 1,038 respondents only five percent claimed to be seriously inconvenienced by most shops being closed on a Sunday; seventy percent said that Sunday working in shops should be kept to a minimum, sixty-one percent that it was nice to have one day a week when the streets were quiet, and a massive ninety-one percent that MPs should be allowed a free vote on the Second Reading of the Bill. Ninety-three percent felt that shopworkers should have the right not to work on Sundays if they so desired.

This re-assertion of the views held by the man in the street, as opposed to the representation of those views by the Government Ministers, consumer groups, or industrialists with a financial interest in Sunday trading, may or may not have evoked the following response from Lord Gnome in *Private Eye*.

It is deeply to be regretted that the progress of the Government's Sunday trading law is being obstructed by a group of backwoodsmen, cranks and religious maniacs.

The law as it stands is a hopeless muddle replete with inconsistency and anomaly.

Critics of the Bill are saying that its supporters are solely interested in the commercial aspect of the affair.

They accuse us of wishing merely to maximise profits by opening all seven days of the week.

Nothing could be further from the truth. Speaking personally as Chairman of Gnome Giant Hypermarkets PLC my sole aim is to provide a public service at, I may say, considerable personal inconvenience to myself, so that those unfortunate people who are at present unable to do their shopping on any other day may now do so on Sunday.

E. Strobes,
pp Lord Gnome,
Gnome House,
London W.1.

There was, perhaps, no one in Open Shop quite as selflessly devoted to the public good as Lord Gnome! But as a group for whose members Sunday trading was a matter of direct financial gain the opposing lobby did have one distinct advantage over the Keep Sunday Special Campaign: available cash. It was simply misleading for Rachel Waterhouse to assert, as she had done in her letter, that we commanded financial support worth 'hundreds of thousands of pounds'. The fact was that our whole operation, run on a shoestring anyway, was fast becoming insolvent. In spite of some contributions from retailers, by the time the Steering Committee next met on 21st March we had been forced to cut back Michael Windridge's consultancy to two days per week, and could not afford to retain Extel's services at all beyond 17th April. The Jubilee Centre was even considering a move from the already cheap premises on Sturton Street to a rent-free office offered to us by the Baptist Union on Southampton Row. I had no option but to prepare a financial statement and once again approach some of our supporters in the retailing industry.

These same retailers were by now well accustomed to my pleadings for public commitment to the Campaign, to which I had devoted a considerable amount of personal time and effort. This culminated in a meeting on Wednesday 26th March attended by top management from Boots, Sears, Co-op, Safeway and Argos. My main hope was that recent figures on the Early Day Motions (Ivor Stanbrook's had now attracted ninety-nine signatures, Ann Winterton's seventy-seven) would be enough to convince the cautious that their backing might swing Commons opinion against the Bill, and that consequently we might agree to draft a joint letter to *The Times*. To my immense gratification this was exactly what happened. Some of the multiples, including a number of famous high street names, agreed to sign a letter drafted by Extel, stating their opposition to the Shops Bill and calling on MPs to vote against it. By the end of the Parliamentary term there was still no firm word from the Ulster Unionist MPs, but on April 1, after weeks of badgering the Home Office about the presentation of the petition, confirmation suddenly and unexpectedly came through that the Home Secretary would receive a delegation on 10th April. I wondered if this was an April Fool until I remembered that the call had come in the afternoon! Immediately I phoned the three church leaders – the Archbishop of Canterbury, Cardinal Hume, and Dr Donald English, Moderator of the Free Church Council – to see if they could make room in their schedules on 10th April to visit the Home Office. Miraculously – and I use the word in its literal sense – they were all available.

Two days before the start of the Easter Recess a question put to the Prime Minister by Peter Bruinvels MP revealed that the number of letters opposing the Bill, sent in since the debate on the Auld Report had risen to a staggering 45,500. This faced the Government with a tactical dilemma. There was little doubt that if the Whips were held off on the Second Reading, the growing revolt on the Back Benches, fuelled by constituency pressure, would lead to the Bill's overthrow. This backbench rebellion could probably be contained sufficiently by the use of a three-line whip to get the Bill safely past its Second Reading and into Committee; but only at a price – an unamended Bill forced through on a three-liner would deepen the rift between the Front and Back Benches, and, if the volume of correspondence gave any clue to the state of public opinion, do serious damage to the Conservative Party's electoral credibility. Michael Mates MP, vice-chairman of the Conservative Back Bench Home Affairs Committee, and as of 7th March the latest signatory of Ivor Stanbrook's EDM, voiced many Members' anxiety when he told his Party colleagues: 'We are offending many of our supporters gratuitously with this Bill'.

The politically expedient solution was to quell the unrest by offering an amendment. But this the Government was failing to do, for several reasons. Their official excuse – offered, no doubt, under the influence of the Auld Report – was that all the amendments currently under review would result in anomalies worse than the 'medieval hotch podge of current legislation' (the words of the *Sunday Times*) and consequently be more unacceptable than complete deregulation. This was not simply bad analysis: it was policy with two motive forces behind it. First of all, and especially since the Open Shop letter campaign had begun (7,700 'letters' by 26th March), the Ministers behind the legislation had always just enough demonstrable support to push the Bill forward on the grounds of 'popular demand'. It mattered little that the opinion polls on which they based this deduction were intellectually suspect and frequently commissioned for the purpose of promoting deregulation; a statistic was a statistic.

Just before the end of the session the Government grasped the nettle and set the date of the Second Reading on Monday 14th April, a week after the House returned. Evidently the Whips had done their calculations, and Ministers were putting their heads down and going for total deregulation, no amendments. Ivor Stanbrook, for one, was ready to take them on; during business questions on the last day of Parliament before the Easter Recess he warned the Leader of the House, John Biffen, that the Government would meet more resistance over the Shops Bill than there had been over the Westland Crisis or even the privatisation of British Leyland.

'You ain't seen nothing yet,' he said.

Chapter 9

Losing in Advance

The fixing of the date at least told us how long we had left before the crucial vote. Granted the delays achieved by both sides in the dispute, it was a desperately tough deadline. At the Jubilee Centre a few days earlier Martin Graham had done a time-and-motion study on our work on the national petition and found the job would take six months to complete. We had tried to speed it up by signing on extra voluntary help, but now that the Steering Committee had agreed to put out the *Sunday. . .Write Off!* leaflet to encourage a second wave of correspondence to the Home Office, these resources had to be split to accommodate another general mailing. When Michael Windridge told me that in addition to all this we would have to send out a final letter of appeal to MPs, to arrive on the morning of the debate, I nearly argued him down. But he stood his ground as he had always done: if we wanted any chance of beating the Shops Bill, we had to put in everything, especially now. As that could not be denied, I duly passed the instructions down.

The Campaign had, as a matter of necessity, ceased to be an exclusively Christian enterprise from the moment we consented to go into official partnership with other groups. That move had been essential, and because we suddenly found ourselves appealing to a wider audience than the church our publications had taken on a less explicitly Christian flavour. Nonetheless at the Jubilee Centre we gave priority to prayer, and this was a powerful force in holding a pretty chaotic operation together. All the way through the Campaign we had enjoyed near miraculous success. There had been no reason, for instance, to think that the Government would introduce the Shops Bill in the Lords, and still less that the Keep Sunday Special Campaign would attract a surge of popular support sufficient to turn a routine piece of legislation into a national controversy. Still, in the middle of what the *Sunday Telegraph* labelled 'a highly sophisticated campaign', the predominant feeling was one of floundering along, barely keeping abreast of developments. We prayed because we knew we needed help.

Easter 1986 saw an escalation in the Libyan crisis. On the Sunday before Parliament rose, 23rd March, ships and aircraft of the American Sixth Fleet had moved south for manoeuvres in the Gulf of Sirte, crossing as they did so latitude 32°/30 – the line which in defiance of international law Libya had claimed as marking her territorial waters and called 'the line of death'. This instigated a series of small military confrontations, after which the Sixth Fleet sailed north again – three days earlier than expected – with warnings from U.S. Secretary of State George Schultz that U.S. forces would take further action against Libya if required.

The trigger came on 2nd April. A bomb exploded on board a TWA airliner flying from Rome to Athens. A hitherto unknown organisation calling itself the Arab Revolutionary Cells said that it had planted the device, describing the act as one of retaliation against the U.S. for interference in the Mediterranean. Three days later a second bomb went off in a West Berlin discotheque known to be frequented by U.S. military personnel: one soldier and a Turkish woman were killed, 200 others injured. This time responsibility was claimed by the Anti-American Arab Liberation Front, but also by two West German terrorist groups. Colonel Qadaffi denied association with either incident, and had actually denounced the first as an 'act of terrorism'; nonetheless in the U.S. blame was being laid firmly on Libya, and by 9th April, when President Reagan went on television news in America to report the interception of incriminating exchanges between Tripoli and the Libyan People's Bureau in East Berlin on the day of the second bomb (a claim simultaneaously denied at a news conference by Colonel Qadaffi) it was clear that pressure in the United States for the administration to 'do something' about Qadaffi was becoming almost irresistible.

British opinion was divided on the wisdom of further American action against Libya. The Conservative Government traditionally took a hard line against international terrorism, and so by implication supported moves made by the Reagan administration to pinch it off at the source. At the same time, although there was circumstantial evidence to suggest Libyan involvement in the bombings, this had not been proved, and some political figures in Britain, as well as a great many abroad, felt that the U.S. was making Libya into a scapegoat for failures in her own foreign policy. With America becoming increasingly isolated over the Libyan affair, pressure from Washington mounted on the British Government to break rank with the other European allies and come out in support.

On Wednesday, 9th April while President Reagan was on American television calling Colonel Qadaffi a 'mad dog', the Conservative rebels were meeting to plan strategy over the Shops Bill. The news had broken the day before – the first of the new term – that Ministers were going to follow through on their threat to use the three-line whip. It had been a close calculation. According to the *Guardian* (8th April):

> Despite the narrowness of the arithmetic, the Government believes it is worth while risking the clash as it does not want to be seen to be giving in to its backbench rebels so soon after the British Leyland affair.

Until now Ivor Stanbrook had been working on two ways of co-ordinating opposition. The all-party reasoned amendment, drafted principally in consultation with Gerald Kaufman and the Clerk of the House, had taken this final form: 'This house declines to give a Second Reading to this Bill, which does not provide for the special position of Sunday, and does not make adequate provision for employees obliged to work on Sunday'. The possible advantage of putting this down was that it might gather wider support than a vote against the Bill itself; the danger was that if it did not, the Government could then use the defeat of the reasoned amendment as a mandate to press on with total deregulation. At the meeting a mood of caution prevailed: with the debate now only six days away it was decided that the risks were too great, and consequently the amendment was dropped.

Inevitably, the second topic on the agenda was the problem of the 'half-way house'. So far it had been impossible to find an alternative to the Shops Bill which would draw enough backing from the Conservative Back Benches to be politically viable. Rather than go into the Second Reading empty handed, however, Ivor Stanbrook proposed a compromise, based on the Small Shops Option, that he knew would be acceptable at least to the majority of the seventy MPs at the meeting. With their approval he then spent more or less the whole night in the Clerk's department so that he could be first in line at 10am the following morning to claim ten minutes of Parliament's time at the end of the month in order to present the alternative as a Ten-minute Rule Bill. This legislation, which he called Shops No. 2 Bill, would not be debated before 14th April, but at least it gave official status to one popular compromise over Sunday trading.

My own preoccupation that Wednesday was to capitalise on the hard-won agreement of the leading retailers to put out a joint statement opposing the Bill. A letter was to be sent simultaneously to MPs and to *The Times*, with eight signatories: Argos, Boots, the Co-operative Union, J. H. Dewhurst, TV Rental, John Lewis, Selfridges and the NCT. Judging that the letter would give the campaign a much-needed boost I agreed with Michael Windridge that the freshly revised final draft be sent to *The Times* as soon as possible. Because we were working against the clock, and because *The Times* was embroiled in the Wapping dispute, Michael took the precaution of faxing the letter instead of using a courier and running the gauntlet of the picket line. Unfortunately the communication reached *The Times* letters editor via his own news desk, from which he concluded that the Campaign had presumed upon his good graces by making a press release before he had agreed to publish the letter. As a result, not only did the letter go unpublished, but considerable embarrassment was caused to the Campaign. Perhaps because by this stage I was feeling acutely the pressure of our situation Extel soon got a letter themselves, pointing out that I did not spend good money on hiring a PR firm to have them ruin my relationship with the Press.

The next day, Thursday 10th April, the Government unexpectedly changed their tactics. Probably this was in response to two developments. Firstly, and possibly as a result of a meeting with USDAW's John Flood, Neil Kinnock had made it clear that Labour, too, was putting a three-line whip on the Bill, and was reported in the *Guardian* that morning to be predicting a full turnout. Secondly, and more surprisingly, it was confirmed that all fourteen Ulster Unionist MPs intended to return for the vote.

Suddenly the Whips were revising their calculations. At the morning Cabinet meeting various ways were once again discussed of ensuring the Bill's safe passage through the Commons. What emerged was a double strategy. The Government's basic position was stated later in the day by Margaret Thatcher at Prime Minister's question time:

'I believe it is common ground that the present law is unenforceable. I believe there are many who share the view that the proposals in the present Bill would allow a straight choice between freedom of choice of Sunday observance and the costly enforcement of the existing criminal law.'

In other words, so far as the central provision of the Bill was concerned, the Government did not intend to compromise. During business questions, however, it turned out that a carrot was being offered alongside the stick. When Neil Kinnock demanded that the Shops Bill debate be extended, and asked John Biffen, the Leader of the House, to use his 'considerable influence to ensure that there is a free vote on your side of the House', the reply came that the Conservative Chief Whip, John Wakeham, had heard the request and would 'evaluate it accordingly'. John Biffen further indicated that the Government might be willing, instead of using the normal Standing Committee procedure, to refer the Bill to a special standing committee, thus allowing the various interest groups to submit their views and suggestions before the Bill went through to the Report Stage.

What these concessions meant in practice was made clear at 6pm during the weekly 1922 Committee meeting. It emerged here that Wakeham, as the Whip responsible for estimating the likely outcome of the vote, had in fact been the motive force behind the revision of Cabinet strategy, and was now the architect of a plan aimed at preserving the Bill against the combined pressure of backbench revolt and a full showing from the Ulster Unionists. His deal was straightforward: the three-line whip on the Second Reading would not be lifted, but if the rebels gave the Bill their support on Monday the Government was prepared to offer a free vote at the Committee and Report Stages. By this he clearly hoped both to provide an escape hatch for some Parliamentary Private Secretaries – for instance Michael Alison, PPS to Margaret Thatcher, who was caught in a dilemma between his opposition to the Bill and his loyalty to the Prime Minister – and to attract enough of the rebels into the Government lobbies to ensure a comfortable win. That it was a tactical device aimed at reeling in the waverers was clear from the nature of the concession it offered: after all, once the Second Reading had safely approved the principle of the Bill a free vote on amendments would be of limited effect. A sceptic would have said it was not so much a concession to those who opposed the Bill as a way of allowing some less deeply-motivated rebels to vote for the Government without feeling they had betrayed their consciences or their constituencies.

Forty-two MPs rejected the proposal outright. Predictably, Ivor Stanbrook and the other leading rebels were contemptuous of it, and said so to the press. Ivor Stanbrook told *The Times*:

> 'It is a bluff. Once the Government has got its vote on a three-line whip on the principle of the Bill it is doubtful whether any amendment which would have the effect of undoing that principle could be carried on a free vote.'

One more significant event occurred on that Thursday. Slightly later than 4pm in the afternoon Robert Runcie, Basil Hume and Donald English arrived at the Home Office with a petition containing the signatures of 737,639 opponents of Sunday trading. This meant that with the USDAW petition the total signatories of a statement against the Bill exceeded a million. Tea was served; conversation was made with the Home Secretary about the social and economic consequences of deregulation. It was a courteous exchange of views between a churchgoer who was also the chief proponent of the Shops Bill, and three church dignitaries who together represented the disquiet of every major denomination, and the vast majority of Britain's 7.3 million churchgoers, at what the Shops Bill sought to achieve. Douglas Hurd's reaction was impossible to judge. But whatever his personal feelings at the confrontation, the Home Office left nothing to chance; as the delegation left to face reporters a press release appeared informing the world that the four men had enjoyed a 'full and frank discussion', and that 'the following points were made by the Home Secretary. . .'

The ink was dry.

The impetus of the churchmen's visit wasn't completely lost; afterwards all three signed an open letter calling on MPs, in the words of Ivor Stanbrook's EDM, 'not to support the Shops Bill unless it is substantially amended to protect the traditional character of Sunday'. The letter was included in a mailing to Westminster, and over Friday and Saturday the Jubilee Centre worked flat out to get it away. Michael Windridge caused a last minute panic by insisting that certain papers be stapled together before they were sent off. In the end there wasn't time to use the postal service, and the letters had to be delivered to London on a motorbike by Nigel Holmes, a Cambridge vicar who, perhaps fittingly, was the husband of Anne Holmes, the friend whose services I had engaged to set up our constituency network almost a year before.

When I went to my local church in Cambridge that Sunday morning I was tremendously encouraged to find prayer being offered for Monday's debate. I didn't realise at the time just how many churches, of all denominations and in every part

111

of the country, had taken the Sunday issue to heart. Many now understood the crucial importance of the Second Reading and were praying for God to overrule in its outcome. It had been a long time since a Government Bill had touched the churches so extensively and so profoundly.

The weekend news was dominated by two main stories. One concerned the now widespread speculation on a U.S. military strike against Libya. The other, the decisive victory of the Labour candidate in Fulham, Nick Raynsford, who had immediately declared that he would take his seat at Westminster a day early in order to vote against the Shops Bill. This was gratifying, as at Alasdair Barron's insistence we had mounted an effective local campaign in Fulham in the run up to the by-election. But the Sunday papers were generally pessimistic about the chances of the Bill being defeated. Lengthy, depressing quotes were featured from Government spokesmen, trotting out the same shallow propaganda that, rather like Hydra, only seemed to multiply the more you cut it down. For instance, David Waddington's parting shot, quoted in the *Sunday Telegraph*:

'I respect the views of those opposed to the Bill, but seriously it must be right that the public should have the freedom to choose how they wish to make Sunday a special day – free from the sanctions of criminal law.'

To the *Observer* the result of Monday's vote was already a foregone conclusion:

Even leading opponents of the measure were conceding last night that the Government would probably get a majority of at least twenty votes. They blamed the erosion of their support on the tactics of the Government's Chief Whip, Mr John Wakeham.

I knew that if this forecast turned out to be correct (and frankly our own calculations suggested it would), making amendments at Committee Stage would be extremely difficult. Ironically, the thought that after all our efforts the Shops Bill might slide so easily on to the Statute Books did not make me dispirited. The only reason I had stepped into this particular breach at all was that I believed God had called me to it, and if in the end the Shops Bill became law I would not feel any sense of failure. Like Gideon, I had only done what I was asked to do. Now that I'd arrived, as it were, at the Midianite camp with my 300 men, the rest was in the hands of God.

Chapter 10

'The Shabbiest Trick I Have Ever Seen'

The reasoned amendment/Douglas Hurd's speech/The guillotine/Kenneth Clarke winds up/Shabby tricks/The Bill goes down.

Alasdair Barron, Chris Townsend, Martin Graham, and sixteen others from the Jubilee Centre squeezed into a minibus the following day to join me in the visitor's gallery of the House of Commons.

The debate commenced in mid-afternoon, to a packed House. The Order for the Second Reading was read, and the Speaker outlined his decisions on procedure.

'I must announce to the House that I have not selected any of the amendments on the Order Paper. More than sixty-five honourable Members have sought leave to take part in the debate, and there may well be others. . .'

Douglas Hurd rose to begin his speech, but there was an immediate interruption from Gerald Kaufman.

'On a point of order, Mr Speaker. There was a little noise in the Chamber when you made your announcement. . . Am I to understand that you have not accepted for debate the reasoned amendment that has been tabled by Her Majesty's Opposition?'

This was the same reasoned amendment drafted in consultation with Ivor Stanbrook, and later dropped by the Conservative rebels. That it had been taken up by Labour and presented as an official Opposition amendment would normally have entitled it to be 'selected' – in other words, moved and voted on separately from the Bill. The Speaker had not selected it because, as he pointed out to Gerald Kaufman, the issues it raised would be covered anyway in the course of debate. This precipitated a series of objections from Labour Members, including Neil Kinnock, who felt that this neglect of the Opposition's reasoned amendment set an unhealthy precedent. Finally a compromise was suggested to the Speaker.

'As the issue refers to a vote which will take place at midnight, would you be willing to reconsider it and listen to the arguments in detail during the debate to see whether the opportunity of a vote may be extended at the end?'

This the Speaker agreed to do, and the debate was allowed to get under way.

Douglas Hurd stood at the despatch box and begged to move that the Bill be given its Second Reading. He began by explaining how the Bill in its original form had sought to retain adequate protection for shopworkers while at the same time removing the 'inflexible statutory restrictions' on the retail business. The controversy over Sunday trading, he said, had so far been 'strong and reasonably good tempered'. However, he went on, 'There is scope for argument about the support for either side. Last week I received a group of eminent churchmen who reported to me more than one million signatures against the Bill. I was able to report to them a somewhat larger number of signatures in favour of the Bill. . .'

At this point Barry Sheerman interrupted; 'Nonsense.'

'The honourable Gentleman says 'Nonsense'. The score available to me today is 1.4 million signatures in petitions in favour and 1.2 million against the Bill,'

But Sheerman persisted. 'Is the Secretary of State aware that only today I have handed in a petition containing half a million signatures against the Bill, on behalf of the Co-operative movement?'

Evidently the Home Secretary was not aware; he abruptly retreated to a more ambiguous argument.

'When all the statistics and polls and petitions have been swapped, two facts emerge, which I believe the House will accept. The first is that there is a very large body of opinion – I believe a majority, although not the most articulate – which no longer believes in a law which says, broadly, that shops can open when people are at work, but not when they are free to go shopping. . .

'Secondly, there is a large body that wants to keep Sunday special, and that body goes well beyond the ranks of regular churchgoers.'

In comparison to much Government propaganda on Sunday trading this last statement was extremely generous; but what he said immediately afterwards surprised me even more.

'Therefore, there are those two bodies of opinion, and many of us belong to both. . . Many of us see no contradiction between believing that the Shops Act 1950 is unworkable and should go, and wanting to keep Sunday special.'

A strategem to gain the confidence of the opposition? Perhaps. He then proceeded to outline the three choices before the House: total deregulation, maintenance of the present Act, and some form of compromise. On the last point it was no surprise to hear that 'the Goverment have not been persuaded that any compromise of which we have heard is preferrable to the Bill'. But this, apparently, was not going to prevent the Government entering the discussion of the Bill in detail 'with an open mind.'

'If the Bill receives a Second Reading,' Douglas Hurd continued, 'my Right Honourable Friend the Patronage Secretary will, in Committee and on Report, underline our open approach by doing his best to encourage attendance and then by arranging for Conservative Members to have a free vote on amendments.'

Several MPs rose. Robin Maxwell-Hyslop reminded the Home Secretary that a division run on this sort of principle had only a few weeks before resulted in a decisive Government victory owing to the use of the payroll vote – a sudden and heavy turnout of Government Ministers. Douglas Hurd was unmoved. 'The freedom of the vote in Committee and on Report', he said, 'will be undiluted and unaffected in respect of all Conservative Members. . .' But Charles Irving wanted the situation clarified.

'Having listened with care, am I to understand that there will also be a free vote on the Third Reading?'

The answer appeared to be no, for the response was evasive.

'The Bill that will reach Third Reading will be the Bill as formed by the House on a series of free votes. It will be the

116

House's Bill as a result of a series of free votes.'

Again several MPs rose. The Home Secretary refused to give way to them but was stopped on a point of order by one of the USDAW MPs, Ted Rowlands.

'Mr Speaker – we have been following the Secretary of State very closely throughout the discussion about whether or not there will be a free vote. Can we, through you, have a guarantee that at no stage will he seek to move a guillotine on the Bill?'

This was not the Speaker's perogative. Douglas Hurd, however, answered immediately: 'I gladly give that guarantee.'

Looks of pain and surprise passed across the faces of John Wakeham, the Chief Whip, and John Biffen, the Leader of the House. This was an expensive concession. To pledge that the Government would not move a guillotine motion in Committee Stage – in other words, would not force a particular amendment to a vote – meant that the Bill could be talked out. As Lord Graham said, 'You want only two people with fortitude and a thermos flask full of coffee, and you can keep the Government's side all night.' Quite literally, five words from Douglas Hurd had shifted the entire basis of the debate: if the commitment was honoured, the Shops Bill would come to grief no matter what the outcome of the Second Reading vote.

His motives were obscure. It could, of course, have been a tacit invitation to the Bill's opponents to vote it out, but if that was so the Government could have picked up more credit along the way simply by allowing a free vote. Whatever lay behind the concession, the reaction of other Ministers showed that it had not been agreed beforehand and as I watched the Home Secretary conclude his speech I found myself wondering whether it had been a simple error of judgement under pressure from the opposition, or whether the visit of the churchmen had critically weakened his resolve.

From this point onwards the Government were in confusion. When the Home Secretary had finished, Gerald Kaufman rose to oppose the motion, and the debate proceeded with a long succession of ten minute speeches from the floor. Outside the Chamber, meanwhile, Ministers were giving swift and anxious thought to the problem of clawing back the concession so blithely given away by the Bill's chief proponent. It was good fortune for them that the final speech promoting the Bill was to be made by an able Parliamentarian, the Paymaster General, Kenneth Clarke, but at 11.30pm even Kenneth Clarke was hard put to assure the House of the Government's good faith and at the same time make the assurance in such a way as to leave room for manoeuvre. Almost at once he was interrupted by the former Prime Minister, James Callaghan.

'I apologise to the Minister. However, before he gets into his stride, I wish to ask him a question. The House was astonished to hear the comment by the honourable Member for Orpington to the effect that, although the Home Secretary had given the House a voluntary undertaking that there would be no guillotine, the Government propose to treat the House with contempt by getting someone else to move a motion that the Government would accept. . . I cannot believe that the Leader of the House, who has such a good reputation, would allow such a gross contempt to take place. I hope that the Minister will give us a clear assurance that this allegation is not true.'

Kenneth Clarke looked slightly taken aback. In fact the honourable Member for Orpington – Ivor Stanbrook – had repeated in the House a rumour attributed to Government spokesmen, that while the Government would not move a guillotine motion of its own volition, it would respond to a motion put down by a backbencher calling on it to move a guillotine. After a moment's hesitation the Paymaster General correctly said that no one but a Minister of the Crown could move a guillotine on a Bill. But as Gerald Kaufman tersely pointed out, this was not answering the question. Kenneth Clarke protested that he should be allowed to make his speech. Kaufman rose a second time.

'On a point of order, Mr Speaker. It is impossible for the House to come to a view on the Bill without a clear statement from the Paymaster General that the promise of the Home Secretary that there will be no guillotine will be kept. If that promise is to be kept, the Paymaster General can solve the problem by saying so.'

After a brief altercation the Speaker ruled that Kenneth Clarke should be allowed to proceed. He took a lengthy detour through the history of the Bill, wading past several interruptions before he finally came to the point. 'How are we to handle the timetabling of the Bill? Unless we have some structure and order in our debates it is possible for a handful of honourable Members to protract any legislation. . .'

He waited for the noise to abate.

'The Government's undertaking is that they will allow a free vote for their supporters. . . However, that freedom has never extended to procedural motions – it had never extended to procedural motions such as closures. . .'

Here was a nice distinction. A guillotine was imposed in advance of a strict timetable; a closure motion, on the other hand, was moved in the course of a debate in order to force a vote. Since both devices had the same effect, of preventing opponents from talking out a Bill, the Government could employ a closure motion in place of the guillotine, and thus achieve its purpose without being accused – technically – of breaking its word. In the circumstances, however, the closure motion did not make a good substitute because it would only work in conjunction with a three-line whip – something John Wakeham had undertaken not to use in Committee. If the Government really meant to use the closure motion, therefore, they would have been better advised not to raise the issue now. That they did so was probably owing to two things: one, the need to prove that the defeat of the Bill in Committee was not a foregone conclusion; and two, their desire to draw attention away from the more contentious matter of the guillotine.

But on the question of the guillotine James Callaghan was determined to get an answer.

'Will the right honourable and learned Gentleman give me a clear undertaking? It would be twisting the House, in view of what the Home Secretary said – and I do not believe that the Leader of the House would do it – if, having given the House a pledge, the Government failed to resist any attempt to move a motion that called on them to introduce a guillotine.'

'I have already given the undertaking that the Government have no plans to introduce the guillotine', said Kenneth Clarke, again evading the question. 'We obviously trust the guillotine will not be required. . .'

This was met with a barrage of dissent. He attempted to explain himself.

'We are glad that the Ulster Unionist Members are back in their place. Let me postulate one theory. The House could be agreed that a measure that had passed through Committee and Report stages was a desirable improvement on the present law in England and Wales. If I gave the right honourable Member for Cardiff the guarantee that he seeks, it would be open to the Ulster Unionist Members to talk out the legislation – although I am sure that they would not – relying on the Government's guarantee that we would never, in response to any pressure, introduce a timetable motion. Speeches about the *General Belgrano*, let alone other matters, could keep us here until Christmas, if I gave such a guarantee.'

Leaving aside the slightly ill-mannered jibe at the Ulster Unionists, this was the fatal admission. James Callaghan immediately rose.

'As someone who has been a Member for forty-one years,' he roared, 'I want to say that if the Government accept such a motion, it will be the shabbiest trick I have ever seen.'

Though it was left to Kenneth Clarke to finish his speech, this effectively marked the end of the debate. The mood of the House was now one of suspicion at the motives of a Government who, having given away too much ground on a controversial Bill, were now trying to retrieve it by means that smacked of downright subterfuge. Accordingly the division for the Labour amendment was won by the Government with a severely reduced majority. Everyone in the House realised the scale of the Conservative backbench rebellion. The climax came at 12.15am when MPs filed into the lobbies to decide if the Bill should be given its all-important Second Reading: the Noes had it by fourteen votes.

The Government had been defeated. The Shops Bill was dead.

Chapter 11

Beyond the Shops Bill

The debate ends/Libya, and the press reaction/Norman Tebbit: Witch hunts and wordprocessors/Why the Shops Bill fell/Beyond the Shops Bill

Before the result had even been announced Labour MPs were standing up and waving their Order Papers, and for a minute or two, despite the appeals of the Speaker, confusion reigned both on the floor and in the gallery. When quiet had been restored Neil Kinnock rose to make the traditional Opposition demand.

'We must have a statement this evening from the Government so that we can get guidance on whether they intend to repeat the lunacy of trying to introduce a Bill in this or in any other Session. The same fate would meet such a Bill.'

John Biffen stood up to jeers of derision.

'In the light of the decision of the House tonight, it is clear that further progress on the Bill is not possible. The Government accept that position and have no plans to reintroduce this legislation.'

It was a phenomenal achievement. We had just witnessed the Thatcher Government's only defeat in nearly seven years of office; more than that, we had witnessed the only defeat within living memory of a government with such a powerful numerical advantage in the Commons. It seemed as though headline coverage was inevitable.

But the next morning the national papers were dominated by another story; while the debate was in progress American F1-11s had taken off from Lakenheath and Upper Heyford to begin the long flight down the Atlantic coast of Spain. The first air strikes on Tripoli and Benghazi commenced at 2am, local time. Within hours a bitter dispute had broken out over the role of the British Government in a military operation that could probably have been mounted from the American Sixth Fleet in the Mediterranean, and the demise of the Shops Bill was pushed back into the more obscure Parliamentary columns of just a few leading dailies.

Such comment as there was generally sympathised with the Government. The *Daily Telegraph* declared the defeat 'a foolish vote'. *The Times*, after taking a swipe at the Ulster Unionists, remarked in language heavy with the popular mythology that had grown up around the debate:

> . . .As for the rest, the Conservative sabbatarians, this was a victory of whited sepulchres, public Christians who put formality of observance before all, policy irrationalists who would sooner see anachronism persist than fairness meted out to shopkeepers, consumers and all those sincerely religious people, Christian and non-Christian, who would ask merely to be allowed to make a personal choice about how they spend their time on Sunday.

For all that, the loss of the Bill was an embarassing setback for the Government. Speaking the next day at a women's conference in London the Conservative Party Chairman Norman Tebbit made the best of a bad job by forecasting dire consequences for the retailer:

> 'There will be increasing pressure for the law to be implemented, and that will mean more prosecutions against more traders earning an honest living trying to look after their customers. I fear it means that things will get rather less convenient for those of you who are working during the week and who want to commit that heinous crime of buying a pot plant on Sunday.'

He went on to say that the vote had been 'won not by principle but by word processor', and that the huge volume of correspondence received at Westminister had really been the result of machines 'pumping out letters to MPs who thought they were listening to the true voices of their constituents'. It was, of course, an outright lie. Word processors could have been used – if they were used at all – by only one or two congregations out of the many thousands that were mobilised to lobby their local MPs. Certainly at the Jubilee Centre we had decided against the technique specifically in anticipation of the sort of criticism Norman Tebbit was now making. Whatever mass produced correspondence arrived on MPs desks did not come from the Keep Sunday Special Campaign.

As to the point about the prosecution of small retailers – of which much was being made in the press – the Steering Committee agreed at its meeting on 16th April that every effort should be made to discourage a witch hunt. It wasn't our intention that anyone should be made to suffer through the Bill's defeat, nor that the law in its present, unsatisfactory state should be guarded against reform. We had only opposed the Shops Bill because it was an evil worse than the one it sought to replace, and now that the fight was over we were anxious to assist in the development of new legislation that would effect a sensible and fair modernisation of the law.

The opponents of the Keep Sunday Special Campaign, who rather than admit that the public did not want to see the Shops Bill enacted, now attributed their defeat to 'some of the most extensive and effective lobbying of MPs ever seen in Britain' (the *Financial Times*), and concluded that we must have enjoyed backing to the tune of a million pounds. It was a generous compliment! In truth, however, not only had we spent little – we hadn't even managed to cover our outlay; and as a result some time even at the celebratory meeting on 16th April had to be given to the problem of meeting an outstanding debt of over £62,000.

The financial problem only served to underline the scale of the Campaign's achievement. In a way that achievement almost defied explanation. There had been so many coincidences – the Government's decision to put the Bill into the Lords, the confusion of the final debate, even the timing of Michael Heseltine's resignation – that it was hard, with the eye of faith, not to see the hand of God behind everything that had happened. Knowing what small beginnings the Campaign had made only a year before, I was deeply grateful, and not a little humbled.

There were an enormous number of people to thank on 16th April; Michael Windridge, Lord Graham, and Ivor Stanbrook, who was with us for the first time that morning; USDAW and the various retailers who had worked within and alongside the official Campaign and whose contribution I was hardly able to assess. But most of all – and in spite of much gratuitous nonsense in the press about deregulation being the 'will of the people' – we knew that the vote had been carried in the end by an overwhelming show of public support. Often this came from members of USDAW and the Co-op and other organisations that opposed seven day trading; but it came most crucially from hundreds of thousands of Christian believers who had been willing, against the odds, to pray, to sacrifice time and effort, and to make their voices heard through constituency meetings and rallies and petitions and letters to MPs. They had forcefully presented the case for keeping Sunday special.

We hoped that when the time came they would do it again.

*

Ivor Stanbrook's Shops No. 2 Bill came up before the House in May, and passed its Second Reading by approximately twenty votes. On succeeding Private Members' Days it was regularly objected to by Government Whips, and eventually fell. It remains probably the most popular compromise on Sunday trading among the Conservative rebels.

Early in 1987 the Campaign Steering Committee agreed to back a common basis for reform of the 1950 Shops Act, and published their proposals as a consultative document, 'The Rest Principles'. Later in the same year, the Conservative Party Manifesto stated the Government's intention of reintroducing legislation on shopping hours if the Party was re-elected. It said: 'The present laws on Sunday trading and licensing contain innumerable anomalies. They are frequently flouted. We will therefore look for an acceptable way forward to bring sense and consistency to the law on Sunday trading.' The Government came back to power on 11th June with only a slightly reduced majority.

During February 1988 leading retailers seeking to have seven-day trading approved in Parliament met to discuss fund-raising. The meeting was attended by David Waddington's successor at the Home Office, Timothy Renton. The group aims to raise £4.5 million for their next publicity campaign. It seems likely that another Shops Bill will be brought forward in the near future.

Other Marshall Pickering Paperbacks

RICH IN FAITH

Colin Whittaker

Colin Whittaker's persuasive new book is written for ordinary people all of whom have access to faith, a source of pure gold even when miracles and healing seem to happen to other people only.

The author identifies ten specific ways to keep going on the road to faith-riches, starting where faith must always begin—with God himself, the Holy Spirit, the Bible, signs and wonders, evangelism, tongues and finally to eternal life with Christ.

OUR GOD IS GOOD

Yonggi Cho

This new book from Pastor Cho describes the blessings, spiritual and material, that reward the believer. Yonggi Cho presents his understanding of the fullness of salvation, bringing wholeness to God's people.

HEARTS AFLAME
Stories from the Church of Chile

Barbara Bazley

Hearts Aflame is a book suffused with love for the large, sometimes violent country of Chile and joy at the power of the Gospel taking root.

Each chapter is a story in itself, telling of some encounter, episode of friendship that has left its mark on the author's life.

If you wish to receive *regular information* about *new books*, please send your name and address to:

London Bible Warehouse
PO Box 123
Basingstoke
Hants RG23 7NL

Name...

Address ....

....

....

....

I am especially interested in:
- ☐ Biographies
- ☐ Fiction
- ☐ Christian living
- ☐ Issue related books
- ☐ Academic books
- ☐ Bible study aids
- ☐ Children's books
- ☐ Music
- ☐ Other subjects